GEOGRAPHY
GCSE Grade Booster

J. G. Wilson

Schofield & Sims Ltd.

© 1989 Schofield & Sims Ltd.

All rights reserved.
No part of this publication may be reproduced, stored in a retrieval system, or transmitted, in any form, or by any means, electronic, mechanical, photocopying, recording or otherwise, without the prior permission of Schofield & Sims Ltd.

0 7217 4612 8

First printed 1989

To
Jenny, Mike and Roger,
for co-operative days and quizzical breaks

Schofield & Sims Ltd.
Dogley Mill
Fenay Bridge
Huddersfield
HD8 0NQ
England

Typeset by Ocean, Leeds
Printed in Great Britain by the Alden Press, Oxford

Contents

	Introduction	4
1	Maps, Graphs and Other Things	7
2	The Crust of the Earth	18
3	The Atmosphere	23
4	Water	35
5	Landscapes	42
6	Agriculture	54
7	Energy Resources	65
8	Manufacturing Industry	73
9	Recreation, Leisure and Tourism	81
10	Transport	86
11	Settlement	95
12	Population	110
13	Development Issues	118
	Index	128

Knowledge · Skills · Values

Introduction

Know Your Syllabus

There is a variety of GCSE syllabuses in Geography, but all conform to the National Criteria and all share common aims. They aim to encourage knowledge and understanding, skills, and an appreciation of values – all in a geographical context. A word or two about these aims may help you to appreciate what the examiner is looking for in the questions set.

Knowledge and Understanding

Under this heading are included:
- the characteristics of selected environments;
- appreciation of the world's cultures and communities;
- the processes, both physical and human, that contribute to the development of differing environments;
- interrelation between people and their environment;
- the significance of location.

It is stressed that the recall of facts, though important in GCSE, is not by itself enough. Questions are designed to test not only your memory, but also your understanding of, and your ability to apply, the ideas and concepts you have learned.

Skills

You may, of course, use the whole range of geographical skills in your course (enquiry) work. However, some skills are specifically tested in the written examination papers. They are usually associated with a range of material including maps, diagrams, photographs, graphs and statistics. These are considered in Chapter 1.

Values

When considering environments, processes and cultural topics, people usually display a surprisingly wide range of personal attitudes, perceptions, feelings and concerns. In other words, their values vary. An issue may be seen very differently by different people. A proposed new quarry, for instance, may be welcomed by some as a source of employment and wealth; to others, it may be a potential eyesore that will destroy for ever the natural beauty of a landscape. Hints at the end of relevant chapters give other illustrations. To meet the needs of this part of the syllabus, you should be prepared to appreciate differing points of view and make your own evaluation of them. Start by learning to distinguish between fact and fancy, and, after weighing up the arguments for and against a particular issue, come to a balanced judgement.

Syllabus Content

Syllabuses in Geography at GCSE, although sharing the same aims, do differ somewhat in content. Differences, however, are much less than may appear at first sight. Much common ground is hidden by variations in arrangement and wording. To give an example: in Syllabus D of the Northern Examining Association, *Weather and Climate* and *Landforms and Processes* are two of seven specified subject areas. They are not so specified in the same association's Syllabus B, which, however, states that "An awareness of the physical environment underpins the whole syllabus." In both cases, Chapters 2, 3, 4 and 5 of this book fit the bill.

This Geography Grade Booster is designed to cover, most economically, all relevant topics at a level appropriate to GCSE. But you are advised to have a close look at the syllabus you are following, for you may be cheered to find that there is a chapter or two that needs less than your full attention.

Before You Get Down to It

1. A number of geographical topics are best appreciated if studied as *systems*. A system is a group of flows, stores, processes. There is input into, and output from, the group. All are interconnected. Change one, and other elements within the system will be affected. For instance, consider the domestic water system. A house contains a range of elements from tanks to taps to toilets. All are interconnected by pipe and in some cases electric wiring. Water and energy are taken in, and the output is obvious. A change in one item – say, a burst or block in a pipe – will have clear consequences.

A factory, a farm, water in the atmosphere, are examples of topics in which the system approach can be a useful aid to understanding. In several syllabuses, systems may be tested directly. They are often presented in the form of simple flow diagrams, and the text – Chapter 6, for example – includes illustration.

2. Location is obviously of great importance in the study of geography. Questions are commonly introduced by "Locate an example of . . ." or "Describe the distribution of . . .". Remember to be as precise and detailed as possible. Hooks on which you can hang descriptions of position include:
- latitude and longitude;
- points of the compass;
- distance and direction;
- major natural features such as coastline, uplands and major rivers;
- political divisions, countries, counties, etc.

Make an appropriate selection, and with their combined use, aim to treat the examiner to as clear a picture as possible.

On Ordnance Survey maps, grid references properly used solve the problem. Photographs are often provided with a grid of squares that can be identified by letters and numbers. Be sure to make use of them.

3. All syllabuses require illustration of facts, ideas and concepts at various scales. Know your examples and use them. Examples from personal experiences are particularly useful. Don't be reluctant to quote them for fear that you might know something that the examiner doesn't. They have ways of finding out!

4. The subject you are studying is highly relevant to the world situation and is as topical as tomorrow's headlines. Keep an eye or ear or both on the media. You will appreciate the frequent occurrence of the geographical topics. These will illuminate your studies and may well serve as valuable examples in examination answers. Current topics figure frequently in examination questions.

5. Consideration of past papers is a useful part of preparation for the examination. It will enable you to polish technique and test your progress. Types of question vary somewhat from one syllabus to another. Get hold of, and make use of, past papers set for the syllabus you are following.

6. Your final grade will depend on your combined performance in course work and one or two examination papers. The demands of the former vary greatly from syllabus to syllabus, and guidance is best in the hands of the teacher. A danger is that course work can run away with time and energy, and lead to skimping on the preparation for the written examination. Find out the relative importance of both elements in the syllabus you are following and balance your efforts accordingly.

7. Revision is a highly personal matter. There is no one way to learn. Some students read, and read again, and yet again; others jot down main points as they read. Some prepare outlines on index cards; yet others summarise into a tape recorder, and relish the replay. It is important that you find the method that suits you best. There are books for guidance, and teachers are always free with good advice. It is equally important that you make an early start to revision, for examinations have a nasty habit of making their final approach at breakneck speed.

1 Maps, Graphs and Other Things

Ordnance Survey Maps

Ordnance Survey (OS) maps figure prominently in GCSE examinations in Geography. The commonest scale is 1:50 000 (Landranger series), followed by the 1:25 000 (Pathfinder). Larger scale maps occasionally make an appearance – especially in illustration of urban features. Do not be put out by the appearance of an OS-type map of foreign parts. The basic principles of map-reading apply – read one map and you can read them all.

Basics

The basic skills of map-reading are frequently tested, and, moreover, are essential if the information stored in the map is to be fully appreciated.

Grid References

These permit precise location of any point on the map. Two sets of numbered parallel lines form grid squares as in Fig. 1. The square is identified by its bottom left grid intersects, i.e. 3726 (note the order – eastings before northings).

To refer precisely to a particular point, such as A:
1. note the number of the grid line to the left of A; (37)
2. imagine that the sides of the grid square are divided into ten parts. Add your estimate of the number of tenths that A is beyond 37; (375)
3. add the number of the grid line below A; (37526)
4. add your estimate of the number of tenths A is above 26, to give you the full six-figure grid reference of A. (375265)

NOTE: In order to ensure six figures, points that lie on grid lines earn zeros, e.g. B = 380265, C = 380270.

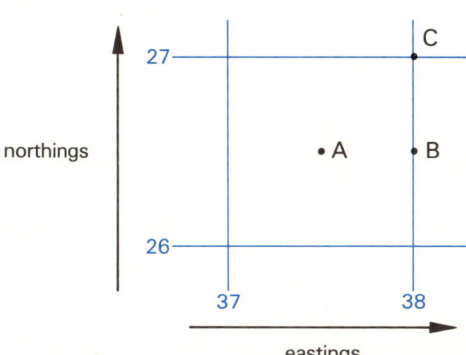

Fig. 1 Grid references

Scale and Distance

Consider a road that is 1 km long. The length it is drawn on the map will depend on the scale of the map.

The familiar Landranger series is drawn to a scale of 1:50 000. This means that 1 cm on the map represents a distance of 50 000 cm (i.e. half a km) on the ground. Thus the road 1 km long will be shown on the Landranger map by a stretch of symbol 2 cm long.

Pathfinder maps have the larger scale of 1:25 000. One cm on the map equals 25 000 cm (i.e. ¼ km) on the ground. Thus, 4 cm are needed to represent a road 1 km long.

For emphasis:
- Landranger   1:50 000, 2 cm = 1 km.
- Pathfinder   1:25 000, 4 cm = 1 km.

With a larger scale, the land surface can be portrayed on the map in greater detail. The fact that Pathfinder maps show every field is illustration of this.

It is useful to note that grid squares vary in size with the scale of the map. The length of side, however, is always the equivalent of 1 km. The grid square, whatever its size on the map, represents one square kilometre of the Earth's surface.

In taking distances from maps, it is not wise to involve yourself in measurement and calculation. Rather, make use of the linear scale. For a straight-line distance, mark the two ends on the edge of a piece of paper and transfer to the linear scale as shown in Fig. 2. Tenths to the left of zero are added to the number of full kilometres noted on the right, to give, in this instance, a total distance of 2.6 km.

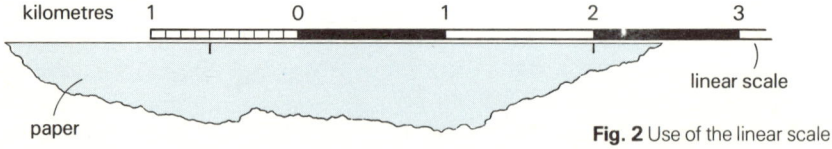

Fig. 2 Use of the linear scale

The use of a pair of dividers is a convenient alternative method.

For other than straight-line distances – a long, winding road, for instance – acceptable estimates can be obtained by several methods.

1. Set a pair of dividers to a small interval, say, the equivalent of ²/₁₀ of a kilometre, and carefully step out the course of the road – carefully counting the steps you take. Retrace the number of steps along the linear scale – carefully.

2. A length of thread may be stretched along the symbol and then transferred to the linear scale (easier said than done!).

3. Split the road into roughly straight legs, and work them consecutively on the edge of a piece of paper; then apply it to the linear scale in the usual way.

Direction

You are reminded of the familiar points of the compass in Fig. 3. If requested to quote a direction in an examination, take care to identify the 'line of movement'. Don't confuse 'of' and 'from'. It is helpful to imagine an outline compass rose located on the starting-point. In Fig. 4, for example, *from* B *to* A the direction is north-east. *From* A *to* B, however, it is south-west.

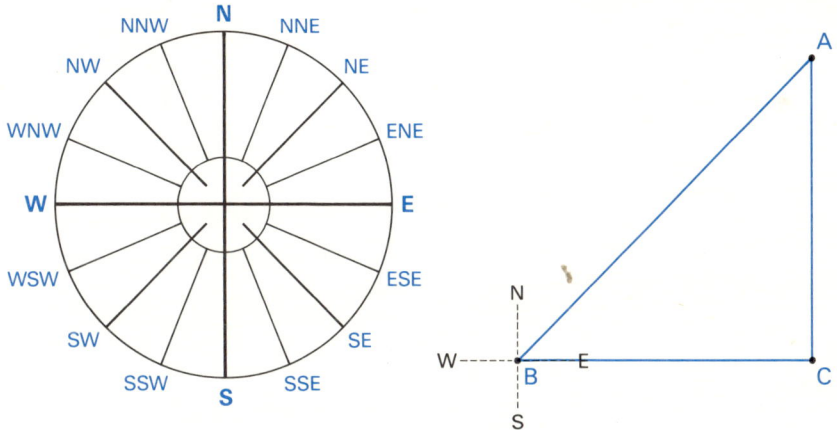

Fig. 3 Points of the compass

Fig. 4 To determine direction, imagine a compass rose on the starting-point

Conventional Signs

A map makes available to us an enormous amount of information about the nature of the land through its use of conventional signs. The key to these signs is included on the extracts used in examinations. Learning of signs by heart is therefore not essential, but familiarity is useful, for it makes map-reading more fluent and effective.

If, for instance, you are familiar with the signs for tourist information, you will very readily be able to comment on the attractions of an area for the holiday-maker.

Other useful groups of signs are:
- land use – woodland, orchard, glasshouses, etc.
- industry – wks (works), power-station, freight line, quarry, spoil-heap, etc.
- rock features – cliff, scree, outcrop, etc.
- coastal features – dunes, sand, mud, flat rock, etc.

Note that in each case the Pathfinder map provides greater detail.

Relief

The ability to picture the height and slopes of the land surface (i.e. the relief) is at the heart of successful map-reading.

The map gives heights in metres above mean sea-level (msl). This is frequently done for important points – summits, for instance – by a dot and a number, a *spot height*. Of dominant importance, however, is the *contour line* – a line drawn on the map joining all points of the same height above mean sea-level. The number and rambling course of many contour lines, especially in maps of areas of high relief, may be a little off-putting, but command of the following points and a little application will soon bring confidence.

Fig. 5 represents an extract from the 1:50 000 Landranger series.

1. We know that every point on the line marked 100 is one hundred metres above mean sea-level.

2. Contours are numbered in a break in the line, and – important, this – the top of the number is on the uphill side.

3. Not every contour is numbered. In Fig. 5 there are two between 50 and 80. They must be 60 and 70. The *contour interval* is 10 metres.

4. Knowing the contour interval, and remembering the way the contours are numbered, we can find the height of any point on the map – accurate within the span of the contour interval. In Fig. 5, point A is 50 m above msl and B is 60 m above msl. C is not on a contour line and its height is best described as being between 70 and 80 m above msl. Try your hand with the other points. Practise on the OS map of your local area.

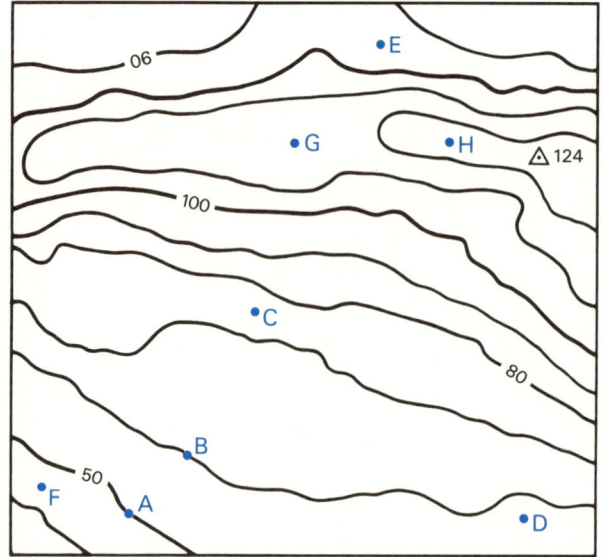

Fig. 5 Contour sketch map

1:50 000

Contour Lines

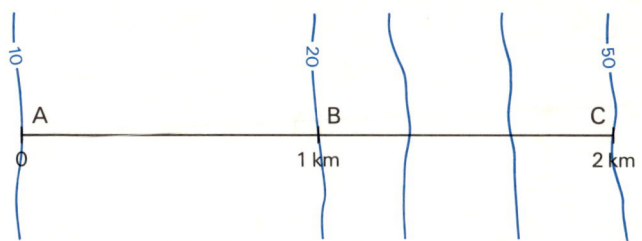

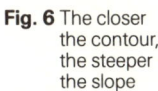
Fig. 6 The closer the contour, the steeper the slope

Contour lines tell us about the slope of the land as well as its height. Consider a journey from A to C in Fig. 6. In the first km, your height above msl will increase by 10 m. In the second it will increase by 30 m. The slope of the land on the second stage of your journey is clearly steeper. The golden rule to remember is: the closer the contours, the steeper the slope. Again, practise on the map of your home area. Try classifying slopes as gentle, fairly steep, steep, very steep, etc.

In contrast to vague adjectives, the calculation of *gradient* provides an accurate measure of the degree of steepness of a slope. Take the first leg of your journey from A to C in Fig. 6. You gained 10 metres in a distance of 1 km (1000 m). Expressed as a ratio in the same units, this is 10:1000 and simple reduction gives us 1:100 (or 1 in 100) which is the average gradient of the slope.

On the second leg, there is a gain in height of 30 m in the same distance. The ratio is 30:1000 to give the gradient of 1 in 33, or 3%.

The varying slope of the land surface can be well illustrated by the drawing of a *sketch section*.

The method:
  i) Carefully examine the line of the section, noting high and low points, valleys and steep slopes. Build up a mental picture of the land.
  ii) Draw a line equal to the length of the required section and erect vertical lines at each end. (A helpful examiner may do this for you).
  iii) At an appropriate interval, indicate on the verticals the value of the highest point on the section.
  iv) Estimate and mark on the base-line the position of high points, low points, and significant changes of slope.
  v) Using the controls provided by iii and iv, sketch in the rise and fall of the land.
  vi) Sketch sections may be annotated by label and/or arrow to locate physical and/or human features of the landscape. This will highlight the all-important interrelationships – e.g. agricultural settlement on gently sloping land; woodland on steep, uncultivable land.

Landforms

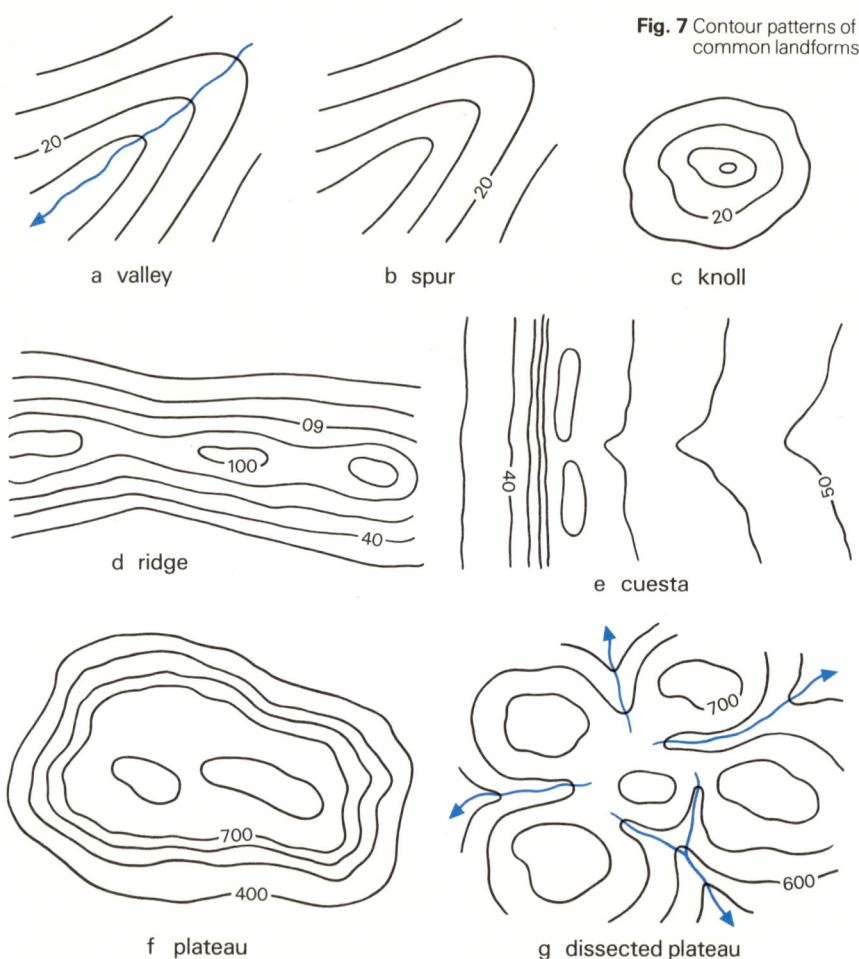

Fig. 7 Contour patterns of common landforms

From the complexity of the contours, certain patterns emerge. These are the distinctive arrangements of slopes known as *landforms*.

1. *Valley* (Fig. 7a). A set of contours double back on themselves to form a 'V' or 'U' shape. The lowest values are in the middle. If a river is present, its blue symbol crosses the points of the Vs.

2. *Spur* (Fig. 7b). The pattern is similar to that of the valley, but the highest land is in the middle.

3. *Knoll* (Fig. 7c). A small number of roughly circular contours are arranged concentrically.

The above are generally small landforms. They may modify the relief of the following larger landforms.

4. *Ridge* (Fig. 7d). A long, relatively narrow, upland feature, its sides indicated by roughly parallel sets of contours. The top of the ridge may vary in width from 'flat topped' to 'knife edged'.

5. *Cuesta* (Fig. 7e). This landform is composed of two slopes of contrasting steepness. The steep 'scarp' slope, shown on the map by a close clustering of contours, is backed by the more gentle 'dip' slope where contours are more widely spaced. Note that the cuesta is a major landform feature and may extend for hundreds of kilometres – only a tiny fraction can be included on an examination extract.

6. *Plateau* (Fig. 7f). A large area of relatively level upland surface, generally bounded by steep sides.

7. *Dissected Plateau* (Fig. 7g). If a former plateau has been so severely cut up by rivers and ice that only a few fragments of the former surface remain, the land is said to be a dissected plateau.

Three Useful Points to Note

1. Flat land can be picked out by the relative rarity of contour lines. The map looks whiter. Fenlands provide the largest examples of flat land. Elsewhere, flat land is rare.

2. Undulating land presents the traveller with a series of ups and downs, usually caused by the pattern of valleys. Most lowland is undulating to varying degrees.

3. The key to understanding is often the linear clusters of contours that represent steep slopes. A useful first step to map interpretation is to identify any such clusters and imagine yourself travelling across the map at right angles to the slope.

With command of these points, and a little practice, you will sharpen your ability to picture in your mind's eye the relief of the land that is shown on the map. For example, suppose you are presented with an OS extract, your attention directed to the course of an upland stream, and a description is requested. Don't rush. Study the map slowly and carefully. You might note that the small stream flows over a wide valley floor of gentle gradient, which is partly occupied by a long, narrow lake. The valley is long and straight, and tightly-packed contours reveal that the sides are very steep, but perhaps slightly less so at higher levels. The great number of contours tell you that the valley is deep – surprisingly so in view of the small size of the stream. Smaller tributaries rush down the valley sides, perhaps with waterfalls in the steepest sections. Precision could be added by reading of the contours to give the width and depth of the valley. In this way you will have translated the pattern of contours into a descriptive word-picture that will be appreciated (and rewarded) by the examiner.

You may be asked for a link with your studies of physical geography. What kind of valley is this? How was it formed? (If the answers have just slipped your memory, check with Chapter 5, page 45.)

Two Landscapes

The OS map shows in detail an area's two landscapes:
1. *The physical landscape* – natural features – relief and drainage, lakes and coasts, etc.
2. *The human landscape* – human contributions such as settlement, transport, industry, etc.

You may be asked to identify links between the two landscapes, for such links frequently suggest explanation. We may note from the map, for instance, that a river is bridged where the flood-plain is narrowest; a town is sited in a gap in the hills; the road follows the gentle gradient of the valley floor; the railway tunnels through a projecting spur.

Further illustration is aided by that important geographical skill – *the sketch map.* This, as its name suggests, is a simple map, boldly and economically drawn to show only the main and relevant features. Fig. 8 is such an example as might be drawn from an OS map in response to a question on settlement. The village is clearly seen against the physical background, which, as the annotations reveal, greatly influenced the choice of site (see page 96).

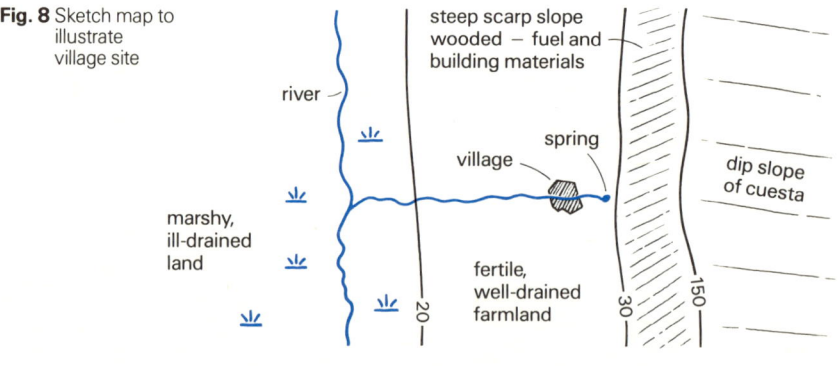

Fig. 8 Sketch map to illustrate village site

Data

The interpretation and use of data is a skill that figures prominently in the aims of GCSE Geography, and tabled data forms the backbone of many questions – on climate, for instance.

Fig. 9 Climate statistics

KAYES 14°N Altitude 61 m

	J	F	M	A	M	J	Jy	A	S	O	N	D	
Temp °C	25	27	32	35	36	33	29	28	28	30	29	25	Annual Range 11°C
Rainfall mm	0	0	0	0	12	96	212	212	144	45	9	6	Total 736mm

Fig. 9 gives climate data for Kayes in West Africa. It may stimulate response at a variety of levels.
   a) Questions may demand no more than accurate reading of the data, e.g. What is the mean October temperature? Which months have the highest rainfall?
   b) A request to 'describe the climate' is more demanding. Be sure to make full use of the given information and give as detailed a description as possible (see page 27).
   c) Identification of links with human activity may be required. e.g. What problem does this climate create for farmers in this area?

Graphs

Data may stand alone in a question or may be linked with other important skills – those associated with graphs.

You may be asked to draw a simple graph or, more frequently, complete one. Can you, for instance, using data from Fig. 9, finish off the graphs in Fig. 10?

In the GCSE you are likely to encounter any of five types of graph.

1. *Linear*
   a) Be careful (as with all graphs) to note and quote the units used.
   b) If one pair of axes carries two or more lines, be careful to distinguish between them.

2. *Bar*
   a) This, vertically or horizontally, may be conveniently subdivided to show parts of a total. This is known as a compound bar.
   b) A population pyramid (page 114) is a special type of bar graph.

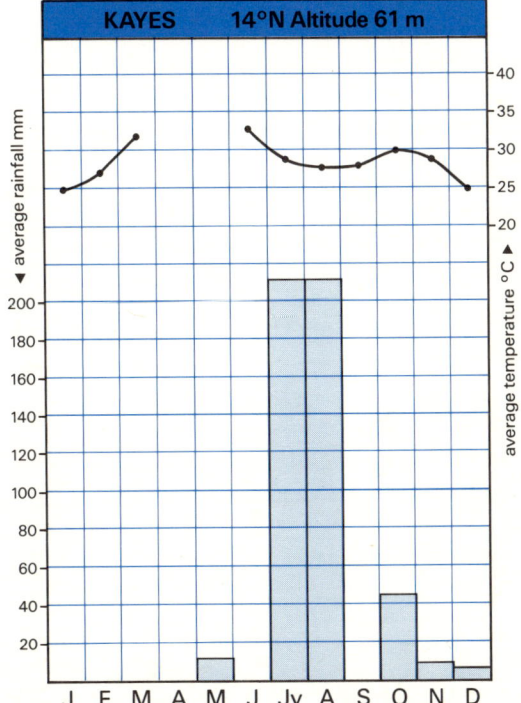

Fig. 10 Linear graph (temperature) Bar graph (rainfall)

Statistical Maps

3. *Circles*
a) These may be drawn proportional to data values, and differences in size give visual impressions of differences.
b) Circles also form the basis of the familiar pie chart, in which 1% is represented by 3.6°.

4. *Radii*

Directional data, e.g. wind, may be represented by lines or bars radiating from the point of observation. Lines may be scaled to give frequency.

5. *Triangle*

This shape is well suited to percentage data with three constituent parts – the structure of employment, for instance (Fig. 11). Testing may involve:
a) reading of data, e.g. what percentage of the working population of Taiwan is involved in Secondary employment? (34%);
b) plotting of information on the graph, e.g. The figures for Belgium are:
Primary 4%
Secondary 22%
Tertiary 74%
Plot on Fig. 11.

1 USA
2 UK
3 FRANCE
4 JAPAN
5 BRAZIL
6 TAIWAN
7 PERU
8 GHANA
9 INDIA
10 ZAIRE
11 BANGLADESH
12 CHAD

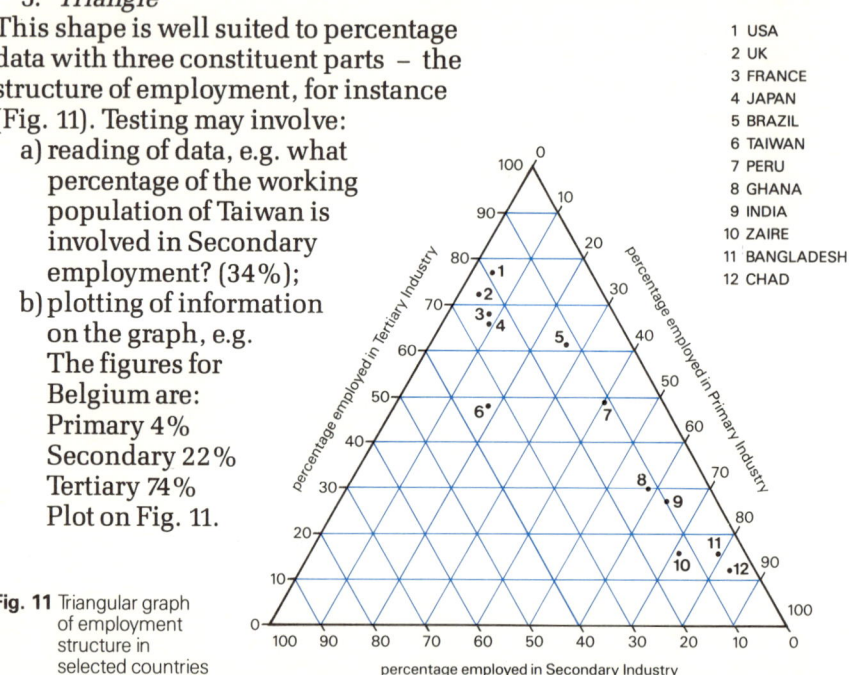

Fig. 11 Triangular graph of employment structure in selected countries

Statistical Maps

These give a visual impression of the variation of a set of data over an area. Common types include:

1. *Located graph*

Small bars, proportional circles, pie charts, etc., are located on a base map – often showing administrative divisions.

2. *Choropleth*

Areas, usually administrative, are shaded to varying densities according to a given scale.

3. *Isoline* (Isopleth)

An isoline is a line joining all points sharing a common value. The familiar *contour line* is an isoline of height. Other examples include *isotherms* (temperature), *isohyets* (rainfall) and *isobars* (pressure).

4. *Flow*
Lines are drawn representing lines of movement, and widened to a scale indicating amount of movement.

In making statistical maps, take care to read keys and scale correctly and quote the units used.

Photographs

Your examination paper may include one or more photographs. They may be of three types:

Air Vertical

These are taken with the camera pointing vertically downwards. The land is laid out before you as on a map, but there are no helpful symbols to highlight important detail, and little indication of heights and slopes.

Air Oblique

More popular with examiners, these give a high sideways picture of the landscape. The nature and function of buildings may be more readily appreciated and details of relief identified. Note, however, that scale changes rapidly with distance from the camera position. The same features – houses, for example – appear progressively smaller. The foreground may be pictured in fine and clear detail but the distant background is much less distinct.

Surface

These are the photographs that you or I might take. They may be used to test any part of the course.

For photographs, experience is the best tutor. Textbooks, past papers, magazines, all include many relevant examples. Don't just give them an idle glance – study them! Don't jump to conclusions. Let your eye move over the photograph slowly and systematically – side to side, top to bottom. Pause at intervals to think, and to query features that attract your attention.

Answers to questions based on photographs are found by clear observation, logical deduction, and, of course, knowledge of the relevant topic. For instance, an air photograph of a lowland area shows a number of fields, each with a regular pattern of dots. A mental trip through the list of possible types of agricultural land use, enables you to arrive at orchards as the answer. Similarly, a photograph shows a large building, dwarfed by a set of huge steaming towers, at the focus of lines of pylons. From your knowledge of Chapter 7, it will be clear that the photograph shows a thermal power-station. The photograph will probably yield evidence of coal storage, transport facilities, water supply – details that will help you to account for its location.

2 The Crust of the Earth

Rocks

Planet Earth is wrapped in a thin, uneven crust made up of rocks in vast variety. Rocks are classified into three main categories – igneous, sedimentary and metamorphic.

Igneous Rocks

Igneous rocks were formed by the cooling of molten material (magma). If this has cooled on the surface of the Earth, the rocks are described as *extrusive* – cooling is quick and crystals are small. Basalt, a volcanic lava, is an example. If the liquid magma has cooled and solidified within the crust, the rocks are known as *intrusive*. Slow cooling can give rise to large, prominent crystals, such as those of granite.

Sedimentary Rocks

Sedimentary rocks have, in the main, been formed by the cementing together of small particles of older rocks. Thus, grains of sand become sandstone, and the finest rock particles become clay. Limestones, including chalk, are interesting sedimentary rocks because they are composed mainly of calcium carbonate.

Sedimentary rocks occur in layers known as *strata*. The divisions between strata are known as *bedding planes*. Strata are frequently broken by vertical cracks known as *joints*. Joints also occur in other types of rock.

Metamorphic Rocks

Metamorphic rocks have been completely changed by heat and pressure within the crust. Slate, for example, is a metamorphic rock formed from clay. Marble is formed from limestone.

Why Rocks are Important

Rocks are of interest to geographers in several ways:
- Rocks vary considerably in their resistance to earth-shaping processes such as weathering, rivers, ice, sea, etc. They therefore greatly influence the nature of the landscape. Lowland areas, for instance, are commonly floored by soft sedimentary rocks such as clay. Tough igneous or metamorphic rocks tend to stand up proudly as prominent uplands. Even the slightest differences in rock resistance are picked out to give the fine detail of scenery.

Rock Structure

Fig. 12 Examples of rock structure

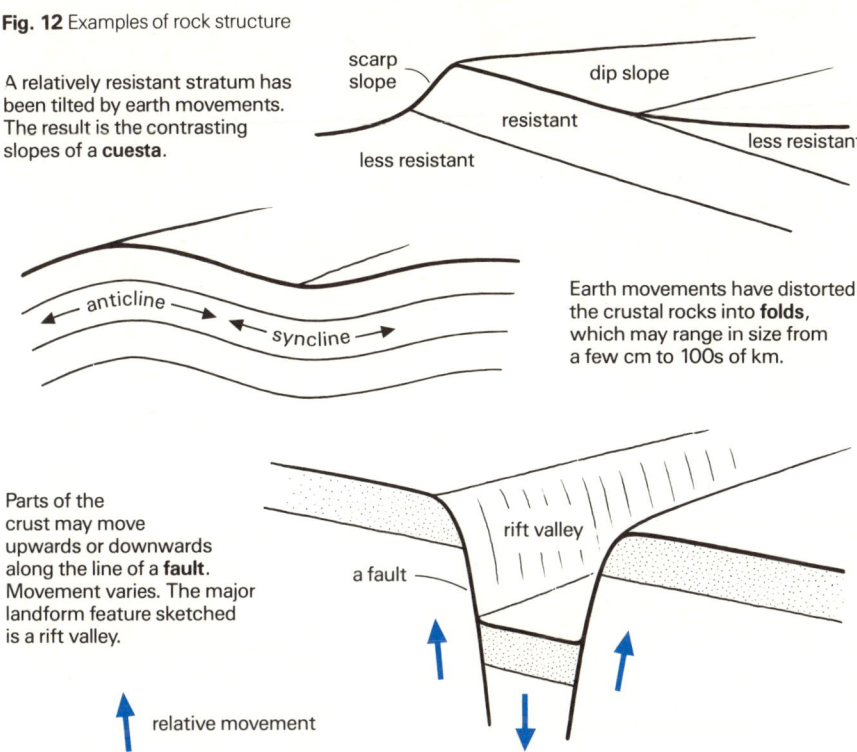

- Rock structure, or the arrangement of the rocks in the crust, is another influence on landscape formation. Some important examples are sketched in Fig. 12.
- Some rocks contain pores or spaces that allow the passage and storage of water. They are described as permeable rocks, and common examples are limestone and sandstone. Permeable strata may be important sources of water, in which case they are known as *aquifers*.
- Soil is influenced by the nature of the rock from which it has been formed. Soils derived from sandstone, for instance, are low in fertility, but warm and easy to work.
- Many rocks are of economic value. Some common examples are:
  coal (energy)
  salt (chemical)
  sand (building materials, glass)
  limestone (chemicals, flux for iron and steel, cement)
  clay (bricks, cement)
  various igneous and metamorphic (decorative building stone, mineral ores)

Tectonic Plates · Plate Boundaries

Plates

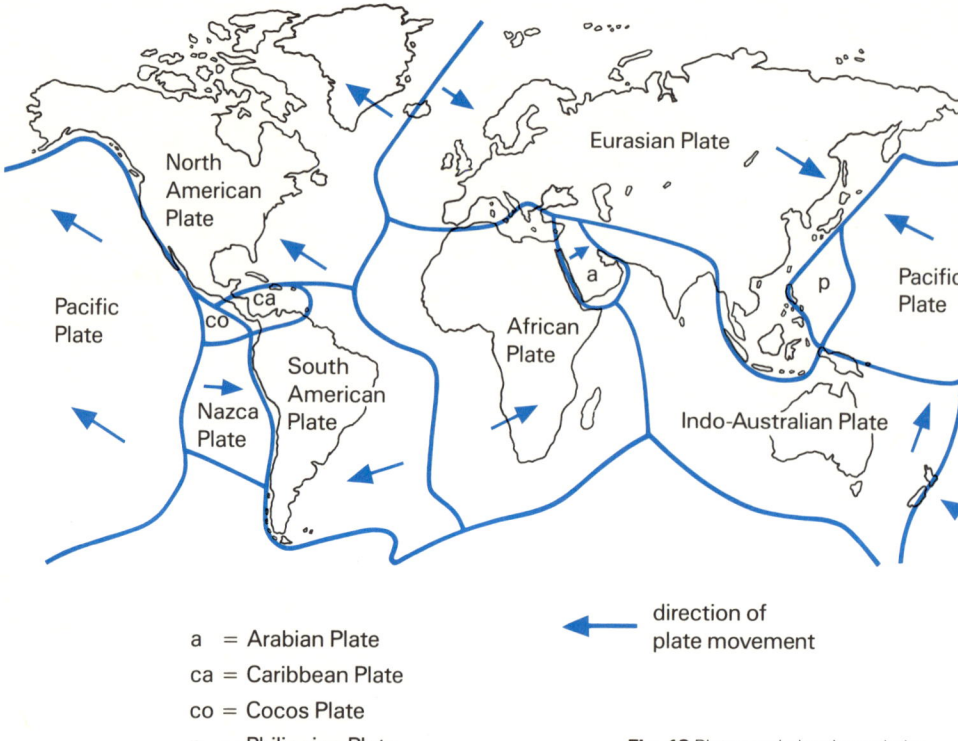

a = Arabian Plate
ca = Caribbean Plate
co = Cocos Plate
p = Philippine Plate

Fig. 13 Plates and plate boundaries

The Earth's crust is split into a number of *tectonic plates.* Major examples are named in Fig. 13. These plates are moving in relation to one another, but movement is very slow – a few centimetres a year. However, the Earth has such a long history (more than 4 500 000 million years) that even the slowest processes have time to produce significant effects. This is certainly true of plate movement.

The crust is active at plate boundaries. Plot the occurrence of earthquakes and volcanic outbursts, and the pattern of plates is outlined. Mountain ranges and the relief features of the ocean floor are also due to plate movement.

Three types of plate boundary (or margin) are recognised, each one distinguished by differences in relative movement.

1. *Constructive boundary*, e.g. that between the African and American plates. Here, the plates are moving slowly apart. Molten material rises up from the mantle to form new crust. It is a process known as sea-floor spreading. The highest points of a mid-ocean ridge rise above the ocean surface as volcanic islands (Fig. 14).

Earthquakes

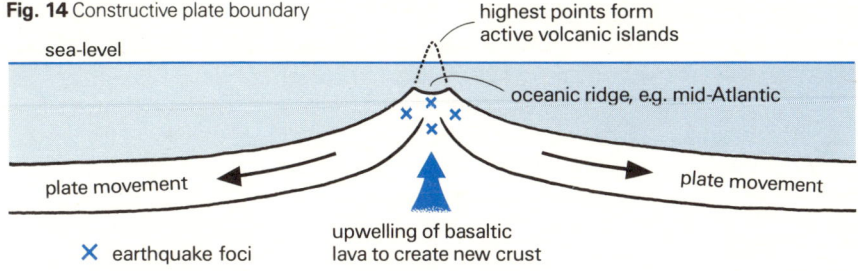

Fig. 14 Constructive plate boundary

2. *Destructive boundary*, e.g. that where the Pacific plate meets the Eurasian plate. Here, the plates come together in a *subduction zone*. One plate sinks slowly beneath the other. Friction is relieved by short, sharp, crustal judderings that give rise to earthquake waves. The descending plate margin is heated and melted and some molten material forces itself to the surface to form volcanoes (Fig. 15).

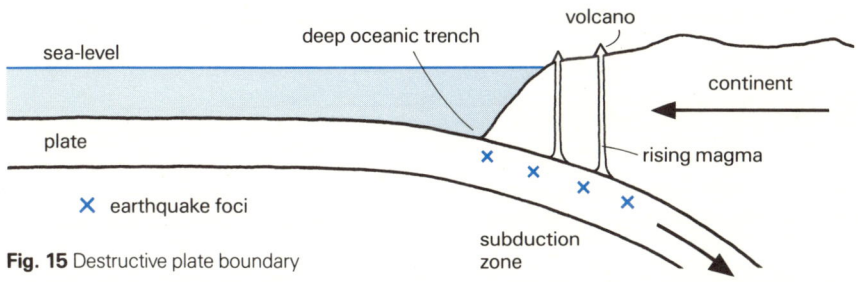

Fig. 15 Destructive plate boundary

3. *Conservative margin*. Along the famous San Andreas fault of California, the Pacific plate slides north faster than the American plate. This causes great stresses and tensions and frequent damaging earthquakes.

Earthquakes

Earthquakes are natural hazards for populations living close to many plate boundaries. They are common occurrences – half a million or so each year. Happily, the great majority are so mild they go unnoticed except by delicate seismographs. If, however, a powerful one – say, 7 on the Richter scale – has its epicentre near a populated area, the result can be horrific. The earthquake in Armenia in December 1988 was a harrowing example of the devastation which can be caused.

During earthquakes, buildings are toppled; bridges shaken down; pipes and cables snapped; and dams cracked to cause floods. The death toll is often high, especially where many people are crowded in ill-constructed housing. Earthquake damage may cause fires which extract a further loss. Interruption of such services as water supply and sewage may introduce a health risk.

Earthquakes centred in the crust beneath the sea can set up great tidal waves called *tsunamis* which may bring death and destruction as they break on low-lying coasts.

So far, scientists have not developed an effective early warning system for earthquakes. Perhaps the best defence against them is to avoid development in areas of high risk. Failing this, insistence on safe standards of building construction is essential.

Volcanic Activity

Volcanic activity is another natural hazard commonly found on plate margins. It can be destructive in a variety of ways. Red-hot, liquid rock (lava) can flow slowly down the sides of a volcano, destroying whatever is caught in its path. The surrounding area can be blanketed with thick deposits of ash and other solid material. A variety of hot, choking gases may issue forth. Heavy rain associated with the eruption may turn unconsolidated ash deposits into floods of mud.

In spite of the dangers, the lower slopes of volcanic peaks are often closely settled, for lava and ash weather down to fine, fertile soils.

Points to Note

1. It is important to know the vocabulary of this topic. It is essential for clear understanding, and the examination may request definition. Ask, and answer, such questions as 'What is a metamorphic rock?' . . . 'a tectonic plate?' . . . 'a bedding plane?'

2. Maps such as Fig. 13 are storehouses of valuable information and are worth more than a passing glance. Don't try to learn every tiny detail, but aim for familiarity with the distribution shown. Always remember a name or two to serve as examples.

3. Process is often the key to explanation. If, for instance, you are clear about what is happening at the plate margins, explanations of earthquakes, volcanoes, etc., naturally follow.

4. Earthquakes, tsunamis and volcanic activity take their place in the important topic of 'natural hazards', where they are joined by floods (page 37), drought (page 32), and tropical storms (page 31). Make a note of specific examples as they are reported in the media and use them to illustrate examination answers.

3 The Atmosphere

The atmosphere is the vital mixture of gases that surrounds the Earth. Its condition changes from place to place and from time to time. Processes are powered by incoming radiation from the sun – known as *insolation* – but note the important point in Fig. 16 that the atmosphere is heated indirectly. The condition of the atmosphere may be described under the following headings.

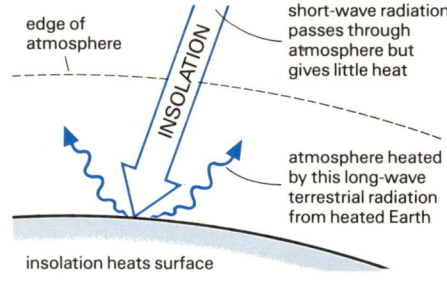

Fig. 16 Heating of the atmosphere

Temperature

This varies with latitude, position and altitude.

Latitude

In general, mean temperatures decrease from Equator to poles, a characteristic explained in Fig. 17. Note that the British Isles, lying between 50° and 60°N, are far from the extremes and are set in temperate latitudes.

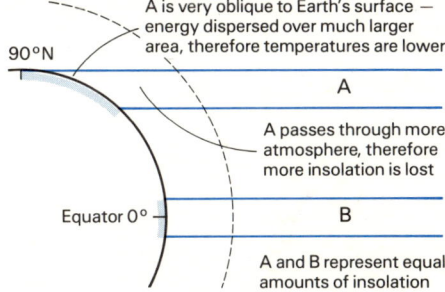

Fig. 17 Insolation is more oblique at higher latitudes

Position in Relation to Land and Sea

Land and water surfaces respond very differently to insolation. Land heats up rapidly but also loses heat rapidly. In contrast, water is relatively slow to warm up and cool down. Remembering that the atmosphere takes its heat mainly from the surface, we have the important situation seen in Fig. 18.

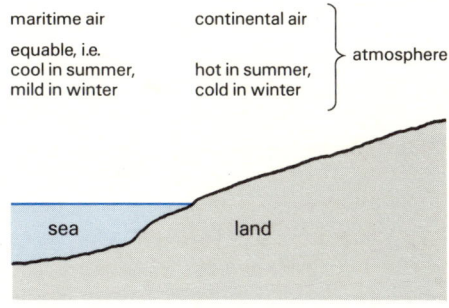

Fig. 18 The effect of land and sea

Precipitation

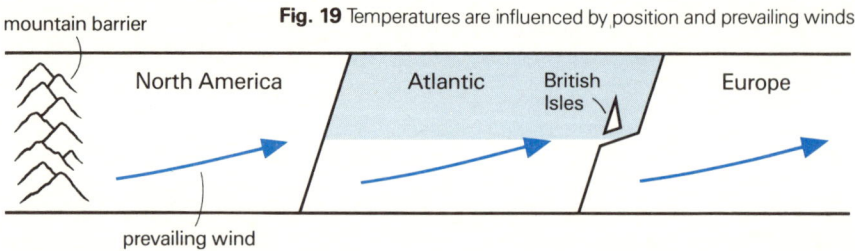

Fig. 19 Temperatures are influenced by position and prevailing winds

The atmosphere is constantly in motion. In Fig. 19, the British Isles are seen to lie in the path of prevailing westerly winds which come over the Atlantic Ocean. Thus the temperature of the air we experience has been influenced by the ocean surface. It is relatively cool in summer and mild in winter. The British climate is well described as equable – free from extremes. Only occasionally, with winter winds from north or east, do we experience a spell of sub-zero temperatures.

Altitude

As altitude increases, the atmosphere becomes thinner and less able to absorb heat. Average temperatures decrease with altitude at a rate of 0.6°C for every 100 metres. Buxton in Derbyshire, for example, is approximately 300 m higher and 2°C cooler than Manchester. High mountains on the Equator are capped with snow.

Precipitation

The atmosphere contains a variable amount of water vapour. Note that this is water in the form of a gas, and must not be confused with the fine droplets of liquid water that we know as steam, cloud or fog. The amount of water vapour that the air can hold depends on temperature. The warmer the air, the more it can hold. When air is holding as much water vapour as it can, it is said to be saturated. If saturated air is cooled, it can hold less water vapour. The surplus is precipitated in the form of liquid water (or as ice if the temperature is less than 0°C). All forms of precipitation are due to the cooling of saturated air. Different ways of cooling give different types of precipitation.

The cooling that leads to rain or snow is brought about by expansion. As air rises it expands, and as it expands it cools. If cooling is sufficient to take the air below the temperature at which it becomes saturated (the dew-point), it rains or snows. Fig. 20 shows three situations which may cause air to rise.

Fog and mist are formed when the lower layers of still air are cooled below saturation point by contact with a cold surface. Tiny water droplets are precipitated and hang in the air to obscure visibility. It is classed as fog if visibility is less than 1 km.

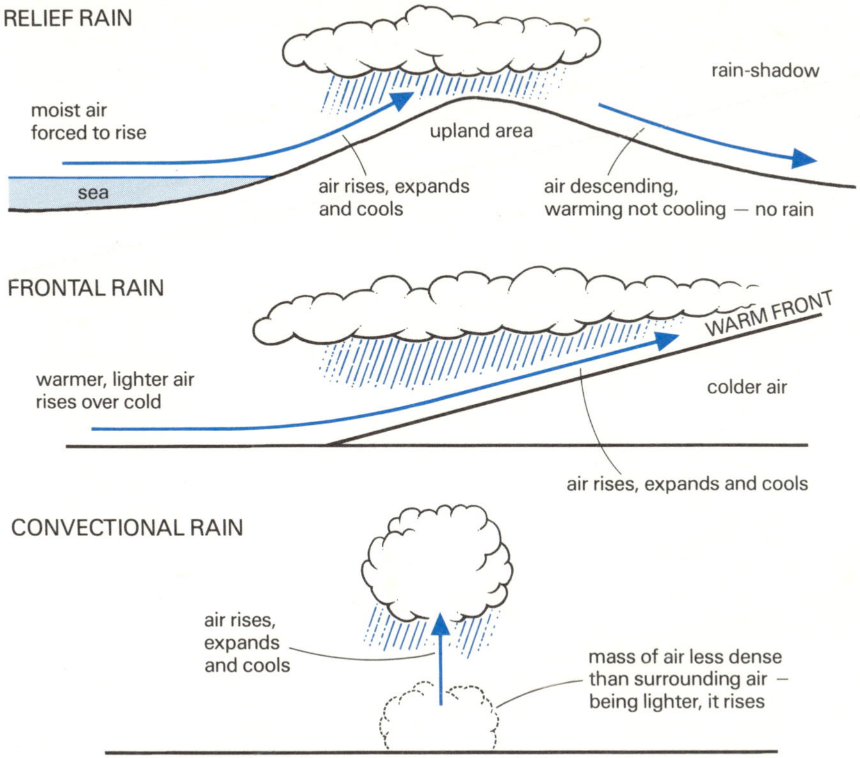

RELIEF RAIN
rain-shadow
moist air
forced to rise
upland area
sea
air rises, expands
and cools
air descending,
warming not cooling — no rain
FRONTAL RAIN
WARM FRONT
warmer, lighter air
rises over cold
colder air
air rises, expands and cools
CONVECTIONAL RAIN
air rises,
expands
and cools
mass of air less dense
than surrounding air —
being lighter, it rises

Fig. 20 The formation of rain

Pressure and Wind

Air has weight and so exerts a pressure on the surface of the Earth. This is atmospheric pressure. It varies with:

- altitude;
- circulation in the upper atmosphere;
- temperature.

Variation in atmospheric pressure is important as the cause of wind. Wind is simply air moving from high pressure to low pressure. Its speed reflects the pressure gradient (Fig. 21).

isobar — line of equal
pressure. The closer the
isobars, the steeper the
gradient, the greater
the wind speed
high
pressure
movement of air
low
pressure

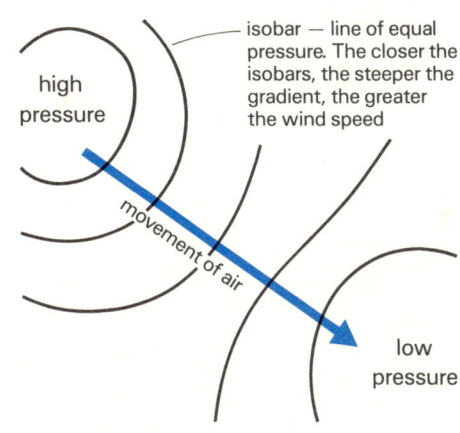

Fig. 21 Pressure gradient

Climate

One area where wind is of great significance is south-east Asia. Winters in the huge land mass of continental Asia are very cold. Air contracts to give very high pressure and cold, dry, outblowing winds. In summer, however, the situation is reversed. High temperatures lead to low pressure which draws in warm, moist air from over the oceans. These summer winds bring monsoon rains.

Climate

Temperature, precipitation, pressure and wind, together with cloud cover and sunshine, are elements common to *climate* and *weather*. These terms are frequently confused. It is important to distinguish between them.

Climate may be regarded as the average state of the atmosphere – the conditions that may be expected to prevail over a period of a month or a season. It is climate we are talking about when we say such things as, "The Mediterranean coastlands have hot, dry summers" or "Winters in Britain are mild and moist".

Elements are measured, recorded and averaged out over a lengthy period of years to give climatic data. This may be presented to us in a table or in the form of maps or graphs.

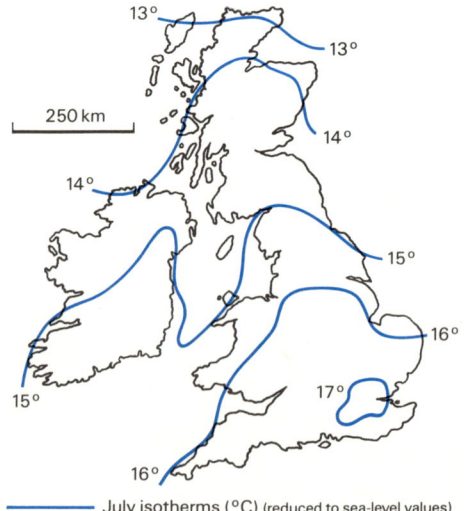

Fig. 22, for instance, shows mean July temperatures over the British Isles. The lines are *isotherms* – they join all places with the same mean temperatures. If you remember this, the detail is easily interpreted. The island of Anglesey is seen to have a mean July temperature of 15°C. The figure for Birmingham is between 16°C and 17°C. London, at more than 17°C, is on average the warmest in July.

——— July isotherms (°C) (reduced to sea-level values)

Fig. 22 The British Isles – summer temperatures

Fig. 23 is an example of the familiar climatic graph. Carefully interpreted, a climatic graph enables us to build up a very detailed picture of the climate of a particular place. Translation of a graph into words is frequently requested. Be as precise as possible. Consider

Equatorial Climate

January and July temperatures and the difference between them, known as the *annual range* of temperature. (To avoid confusion, remember that *diurnal range* is the difference between day and night temperatures.) For precipitation, describe both the total amount and the seasonal distribution.

Graphs record the great differences in world climates. This is high-lighted by the four examples included below. Test yourself by writing descriptions of the climate of each. Examination questions frequently request explanation as well as description. This chapter provides the material for the answers. Suggestions are given alongside each graph.

Equatorial

Low latitude – concentrated insolation – high temperatures. Little seasonal variation in insolation or temperature. With high temperatures and moist air – heavy daily convectional showers – much rain all year round.

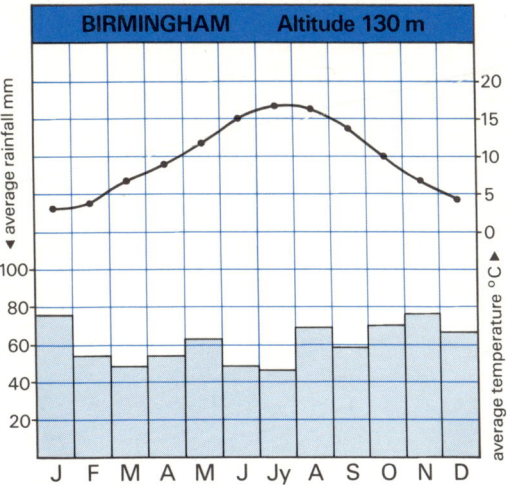

Fig. 23 Climate graph of Birmingham

Fig. 24 Equatorial climate

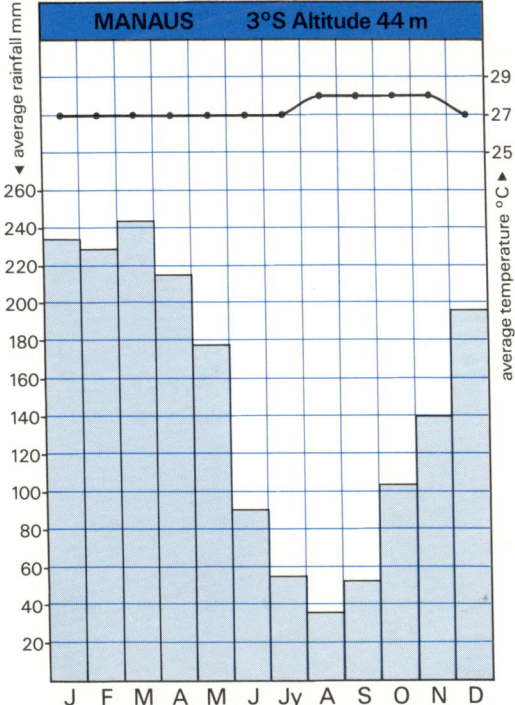

Monsoon Climate · Continental Climate

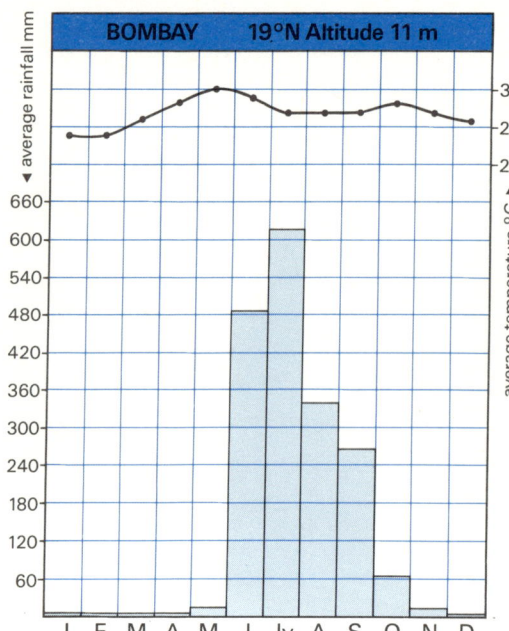

Fig. 25 Monsoon climate

Monsoon

Low latitudes – high temperature. Slight dip in temperatures due to cloud associated with rainy season. Marked seasonal contrast in rainfall – monsoonal reversal of wind direction.

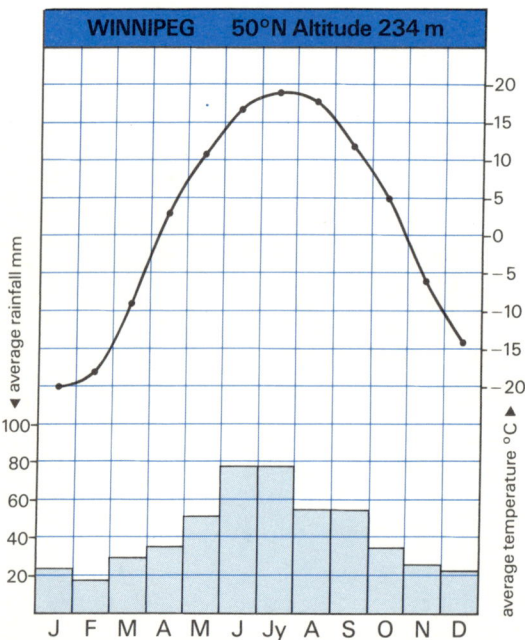

Fig. 26 Continental climate

Continental

Centre of large landmass – continental conditions of hot summers and cold winters, hence large annual range of temperature. Far from ocean and mountain barrier – low mean precipitation (snow in winter). Summer maximum of precipitation – summer convectional showers.

Mediterranean Climate · Weather

Fig. 27 Mediterranean climate

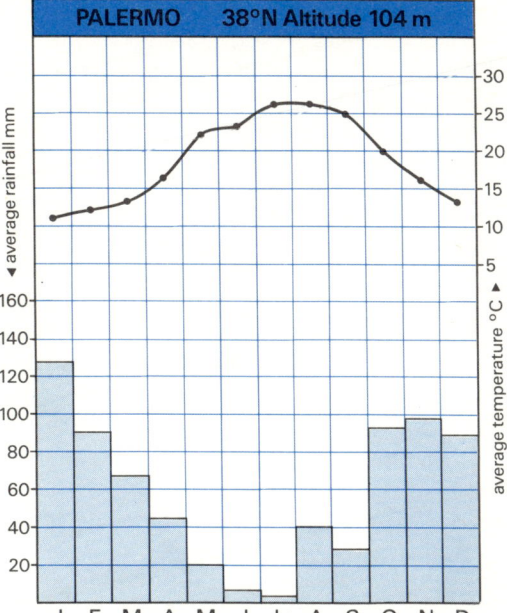

Mediterranean

In summer, region dominated by high-pressure conditions – hot, dry and sunny. In winter, low-pressure conditions prevail and depressions (page 30) bring moisture.

Weather

Weather is the state of the atmosphere at a particular time of short duration. It is weather we are talking about when we make such statements as, "It's a nice day today", or "It looks like rain". Weather is variable – nowhere more so than over the British Isles.

Examine Fig. 28. We experience a short spell of one type of weather when an air mass, with characteristics gained from conditions in its source area, extends over the British Isles. When one air mass retreats, it is replaced by another which brings a short spell of different weather. Polar Maritime and Tropical Maritime dominate British weather for most of the time. The others are only infrequent visitors.

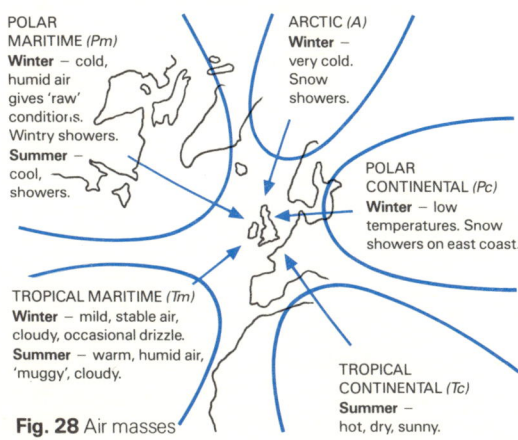

POLAR MARITIME *(Pm)*
Winter – cold, humid air gives 'raw' conditions. Wintry showers.
Summer – cool, showers.

ARCTIC *(A)*
Winter – very cold. Snow showers.

POLAR CONTINENTAL *(Pc)*
Winter – low temperatures. Snow showers on east coast.

TROPICAL MARITIME *(Tm)*
Winter – mild, stable air, cloudy, occasional drizzle.
Summer – warm, humid air, 'muggy', cloudy.

TROPICAL CONTINENTAL *(Tc)*
Summer – hot, dry, sunny.

Fig. 28 Air masses

Fronts

Day to day, or even hour to hour, weather variations are mainly due to the influence of weather systems carried within the circulation of the lower atmosphere, especially depressions (lows), but also anticyclones (highs).

Fig. 29 sketches the characteristic features of the depression that is such a frequent visitor to our daily weather maps. It is important to appreciate that the depression is not as flat as the surface of the page. It is a three-dimensional chunk of the atmosphere, perhaps a thousand kilometres across. The sketch shows the surface position of the fronts. The warm front, for example, inclines gently up to the right.

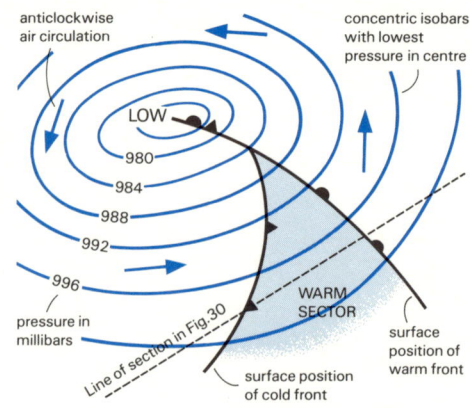

Fig. 29 Chart of a typical depression (low)

The whole circulating mass of air that makes up a typical depression reaches the British Isles from over the Atlantic, and drifts away eastwards.

It is at the fronts that weather changes occur. Fig. 20 (page 25) explains why rain is formed on the warm front. The cold front also brings rain, as the advancing cold air forces upwards the warm, moist air of the warm sector. Put the two cross-sections together and we have Fig. 30, which gives the cross-section of a typical depression. This shows the familiar sequence of weather changes that we experience with the passage of a depression. Watch out for the next one passing over – warning can be obtained from the television weather forecasts, or from newspapers.

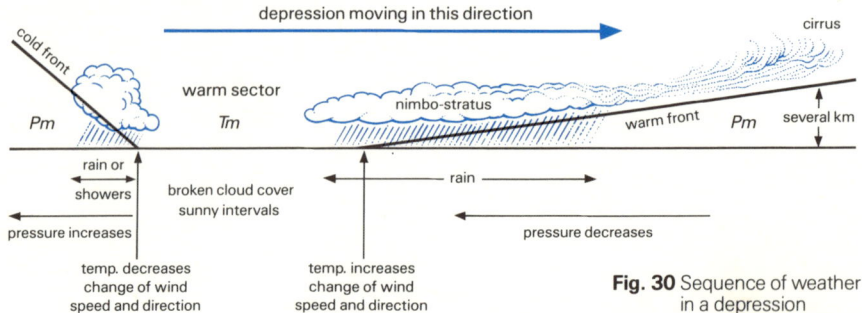

Fig. 30 Sequence of weather in a depression

An *anticyclone* is mapped in Fig. 31. Air is descending, being warmed rather than cooled, hence skies are usually clear and there is little chance of rain. Temperatures vary with the season.

Summer:

With long hours of strong insolation and clear skies, temperatures build up to high levels.

Winter:

Loss of heat at night is greater than the input during the few hours of daylight, when insolation is very oblique and ineffective. Temperatures become low and frost is frequent. When air is sufficiently moist, the cooling of the surface under high-pressure conditions commonly leads to fog or mist.

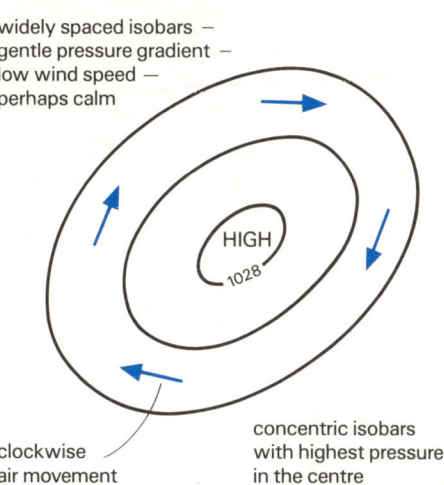

Fig. 31 An anticyclone or 'high'

widely spaced isobars —
gentle pressure gradient —
low wind speed —
perhaps calm

clockwise air movement

concentric isobars with highest pressure in the centre

Environmental Hazards

Exceptional circumstances see the atmosphere in dangerous and damaging moods.

Wind

The high temperatures and humidity of the air over tropical oceans fuel powerful storms known as *cyclones* in the Indian Ocean, *hurricanes* in the West Indies, and *typhoons* in the Pacific. These storms are typically 100 km to 400 km across. At the centre is a small 'eye' of extremely low pressure and quiet weather. Away from the eye, a very steep pressure gradient gives wind speeds of 250 km/h or more. The whole wildly whirling mass of air, cloud and rain moves inland at a speed of about 20 km/h.

These tropical storms can be devastating, and nowhere more so than in Bangladesh, a country prone to natural disasters. The cyclone brings serious loss of life and vast damage to buildings and agriculture by:

- high winds;
- torrential rain;
- flooding;
- storm surge. In coastal regions, this may be the most damaging effect. South Bangladesh is low delta land just a metre or so above mean sea-level. Incoming strong winds drag up the level of the sea and salt water surges over the land, carrying all before it. In extreme cases, thousands of lives may be lost;
- General destruction causes health hazards, e.g. by pollution of water supplies.

Tornadoes are small, short-lived, but intensely powerful storms most commonly experienced in the central states of the USA. Pressure at the centre is so low that buildings may explode outwards. Winds of more than 500 km/h may be experienced. It is impossible to be sure of these speeds, for, like everything else in the narrow, short and winding path of the tornado, anemometers are destroyed.

Rainfall (and lack of it)

Heavy rainfall obviously contributes to the environmental hazards of *floods* and *landslides*.

In contrast, drought is a serious hazard in some climates. The danger is greatest in areas of low and fluctuating rainfall. The African Sahel, the zone south of the Sahara from the Atlantic to Ethiopia, provides a recurring and painful example. The 1980s saw a series of years with rainfall well below the average. Rivers ceased to flow, the water-table fell, and wells ran dry. Crops failed and livestock died. Famine was widespread and many thousands of people starved to death.

The consequences of serious and persistent drought such as that of the Sahel may be very long-lasting. In conditions of drought, starving livestock may destroy every scrap of vegetation. There remains nothing to protect the dry, dusty soil from the wind. The finest, most fertile component is blown away in dust-storms. Coarser material is piled up in sand-dunes. The land is now virtually a desert. This process is known as *desertification*. The loss of the heart of the soil makes recovery a long and slow process when the rains return.

Human Influences on the Atmosphere

People are greatly and variously influenced by the many moods of the atmosphere, but, surprisingly perhaps, the atmosphere can be influenced by people. The *heat island effect* is one small example. The temperatures over a major city are commonly between 1°C and 3°C warmer than over the surrounding countryside. There are two main reasons:

1. Buildings and dark road surfaces readily absorb insolation, are warmed, and radiate heat to the urban atmosphere.

2. Domestic and industrial heating, car exhausts, etc. are a further slight warming influence.

Other examples of the influence of built-up areas on weather and climate include:

- Fog plus smoke and other pollutants produce *smog*.
- Friction with buildings reduces wind speed, though local funnelling may give high velocities.
- Rainfall may be greater through more frequent convectional showers.

Air Pollution

A most topical human impact on the atmosphere is *air pollution*. The air receives pollutants – both solid particles and waste gases – and because the atmosphere is in constant complex circulation, nowhere is entirely free from their influence. In certain situations, air pollution is dangerously concentrated.

Mexico City is an example:
- Over 100 000 factories and 3 million cars pump pollutants into the atmosphere.
- Little money is available for pollution control.
- Mexico City is ringed by mountains that act as a trap for pollutants.
- At an altitude of 2255 m, the oxygen level is naturally low, hence pollution is more serious. Pollutants have difficulty in escaping because of the high basin nature of Mexico City's situation. They hang in the thin air, greatly impair visibility, and cause damage to buildings, crops and vegetation. More serious, however, is the health hazard. It has been said that just to breathe the air is as dangerous as smoking 40 cigarettes a day. There is, understandably, a high death rate from respiratory diseases.

Acid Rain

Acid rain is another topical pollution problem. Rain is naturally acidic. It has an average pH value of 5.6 (pH7 is neutral). (This is because rain combines with carbon dioxide present in the atmosphere to form carbonic acid.) When the pH of rain falls below 5.6, we talk of acid rain and worry about its effects.

It is the release of pollutants into the atmosphere that causes increased acidity, and hence acid rain. The burning of coal (today largely in thermal power-stations) gives off sulphur dioxide and nitrogen oxide. The latter is also a major component of car exhaust fumes. These gases combine with water vapour to give sulphuric acid and nitric acid. As a result, rain commonly has a pH of between 4.5 and 4.0. An extreme value of pH2.4 (slightly less acidic than vinegar) has been recorded. Winds may take the pollution far from its source area. Scandinavia, to windward of the United Kingdom, suffers greatly from:
- Destruction of fish and plant life in lakes.
- Increased acidity of soils.
- Forest trees being seriously damaged.
- Increased weathering of buildings.
- Increased acidity of water supplies.

To check the emission of pollutants into the atmosphere is a long and costly business even for the rich industrialised countries of the world. Many have made a start, however, by, for instance, fitting filters in power-station chimneys to extract the sulphur.

Points to Note

1. The atmosphere may be tested directly, with an enthusiasm that varies from syllabus to syllabus. But, for all syllabuses, it is important to appreciate the influence of the atmosphere on all manner of geographical topics. In the course of your studies, look out for – and take good note of – such relationships. For instance:
   a) The reason why holidaymakers flood to Mediterranean coastlands in summer is evident from the climate graph Fig. 27, page 29.
   b) The life of the farmer in south-east Asia is greatly influenced by the climate summarised in Fig. 25.

2. Be sure that you can translate graphs and data into verbal descriptions of climate. Use the term 'mean' to emphasise that climate is concerned with the average condition of the atmosphere.

3. Develop a clear picture of the climate of the UK so that you can make sound comparisons with climates in other parts of the world.

4. When challenged with a climate graph, or data, first check which month has the highest mean temperature. If it is January, the graph is of a place in the southern hemisphere, where seasons are reversed. Incidentally, be careful with the word 'season'. The pattern typical of the UK is not found in many other parts of the world. In Monsoon (page 28) and Tropical Continental (page 14) areas, 'wet' and 'dry' respectively are more appropriate terms.

5. Weather, too, influences people. Fog, snow and ice, for example, can cause havoc with transport. Note the ways in which people try to defend themselves, e.g. wind-breaks, the planting of orchards on slopes, etc.

6. If weather features prominently in your syllabus, the television weather forecasts, with their weather charts and satellite photographs, are most helpful.

7. Fig. 29, page 30, is the key to questions that require a prediction of changes in the weather.

8. Storms, drought, etc. link up with other natural hazards such as earthquakes and volcanic eruptions to form an important component of many syllabuses.

4 Water

The Hydrological Cycle

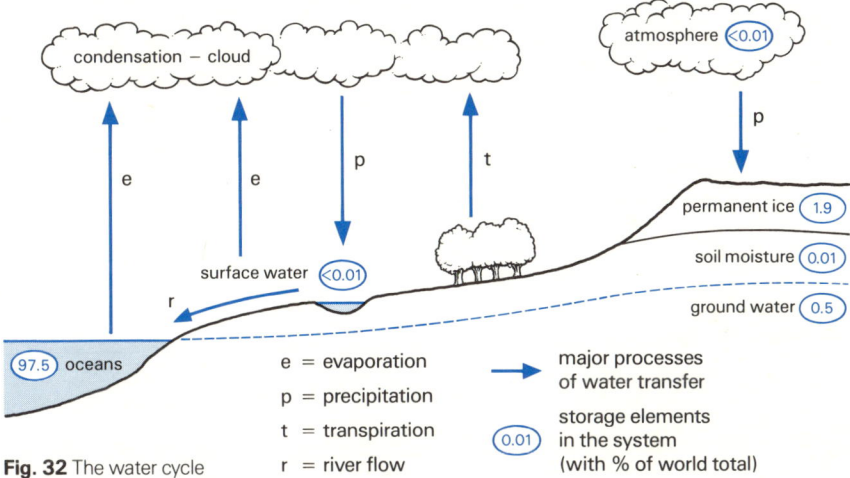

Fig. 32 The water cycle

e = evaporation
p = precipitation
t = transpiration
r = river flow

→ major processes of water transfer

(0.01) storage elements in the system (with % of world total)

The Earth's crust and atmosphere are linked in the water (hydrological) cycle (Fig. 32). It is a system powered by energy from the sun. The water cycle is described as a *closed* system because there is no gain or loss of water – there is a fixed amount in circulation.

The river basin is the unit of study of the land section of the water cycle. Its main features are seen in Fig. 33. The *watershed* is the line of highest land that forms the boundary of the basin. Every drop of water that falls on the basin (unless lost by evaporation or transpiration) makes its way by various routes to the outlet of the basin, which may be a larger river or the sea.

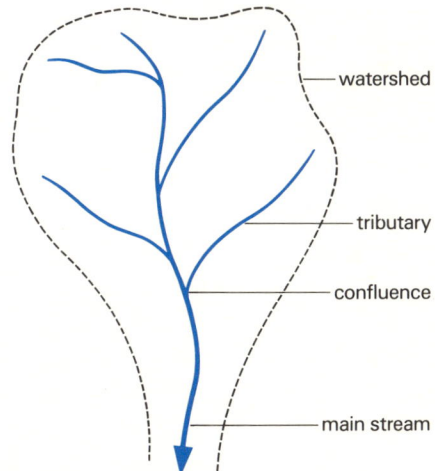

Fig. 33 A river basin

Infiltration

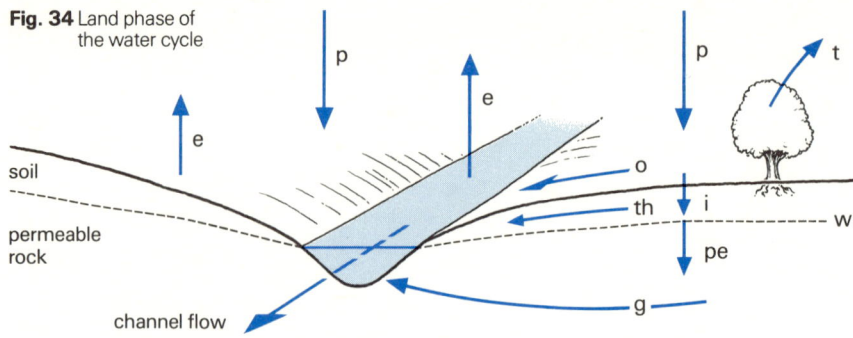

Fig. 34 Land phase of the water cycle

Fig. 34 gives a close-up view of the important land phase of the water cycle. The meaning of the letters e, p and t will be familiar from Fig. 32, but look at the new items:

- i = infiltration – of water into the soil.
- pe = percolation – only if the rock is permeable, of course.
- w = water table – the level below which the permeable rock is saturated.
- o = overland flow.
- th = through-flow.
- g = groundwater flow.

The three types of flow vary greatly in speed. Overland flow is by far the quickest. Groundwater flow is very, very slow.

Infiltration is at the heart of the system. Under natural conditions, the rain as it falls is absorbed by the soil and moves slowly under the surface, eventually to reach the river channel. This is not always the case. If rainfall is intense, as in a thunderstorm, for instance, the rate of rainfall may be greater than the rate at which it can infiltrate into the soil. The surplus – the rain that cannot get into the soil – moves rapidly over the surface as overland flow. Also, if soil is saturated from earlier rain, the rate of infiltration is low, and even quite gentle rain gives quick overland flow. Frozen soils produce the same effect. Built-up areas, with their impermeable surfaces and fast gutters and drains, also rapidly direct rainwater to rivers.

Quick delivery by overland flow leads to a rapid rise in the level of water in the river channel. When the level rises above the height of the bank, a flood results.

The *discharge* of a river (the volume of water that passes per second) varies greatly with time. Change is illustrated by a *hydrograph* such as the example given in Fig. 35. The inset graph records the rainfall event – and the main curve shows how the river responds. A large amount of overland flow will give a steep rise as illustrated. If delivery is by slower through-flow, the rise will be more gentle and peak discharge much lower.

Fig. 35 A storm hydrograph

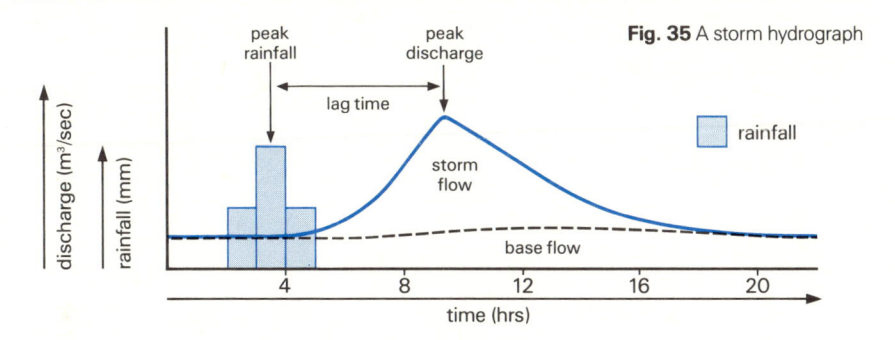

The hydrograph must be distinguished from the graph of a river's *regime* such as Fig. 36. This gives the river's average monthly discharge. In some climatic regions, the pattern of discharge is very uneven. In areas of heavy and seasonal rainfall (monsoon lands, for example), or in cold climates where winter snows melt rapidly in spring, discharge may be seasonally very high, and result in regular flooding.

Fig. 36 Graph of a river regime

Flooding

Flooding is a natural hazard that ranks with those considered in Chapters 2 and 3. When the discharge becomes greater than channel capacity, water spills over on to flanking land. In major floods, farmland is inundated and crops are ruined; buildings are damaged or destroyed; bridges are swept away and communications interrupted. Lives may be lost either directly or through disease. The risk to life is greatest in lands along the great rivers of south-east Asia, such as the Hwang Ho (China), the Ganges (India), or the Brahmaputra (Bangladesh), where the fertile but low-lying flood-plains support a high-density of farming population.

Preventing Disaster

Flooding is a natural phenomenon, but the consequences of human activities can make it both more frequent and more serious. Urban development, by introducing impermeable surfaces and quick-flow gutters and drains, is one example. Far more serious, however, is the

Water Distribution

sequence of events, common in many parts of the Third World, illustrated in Fig. 37.

Measures that may be taken to reduce the hazards of damaging floods include:
- planting trees;
- constructing storage reservoirs;
- straightening the river channel to increase the speed of flow;
- widening and deepening the channel.

Such measures are costly. In many poor countries where the hazards are greatest and the wealth is least, large populations can do little more than accept the risk and endure the consequences.

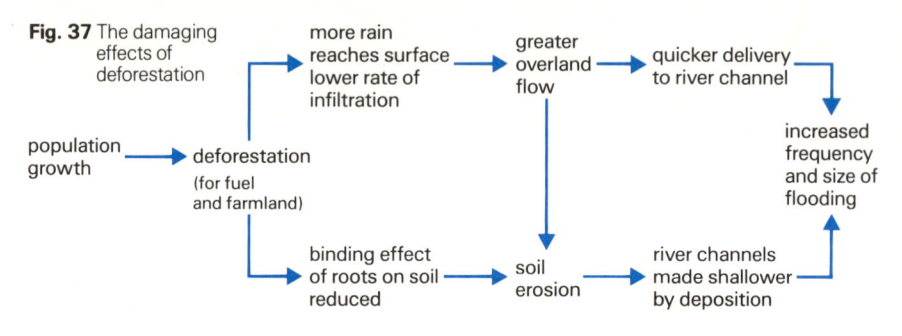

Fig. 37 The damaging effects of deforestation

```
population growth → deforestation (for fuel and farmland)
    ├→ more rain reaches surface, lower rate of infiltration → greater overland flow → quicker delivery to river channel → increased frequency and size of flooding
    └→ binding effect of roots on soil reduced → soil erosion → river channels made shallower by deposition → increased frequency and size of flooding
```

Distribution

Water is a natural resource vital for agriculture, industry, communication and domestic purposes. Its distribution is uneven in space and time. Arid and semi-arid areas clearly suffer from serious shortages; but even in relatively well-watered areas, an exceptionally dry year can bring the problem of drought. The quality of water supply also varies. In advanced Western countries, for instance, pure, clean water is available at the turn of a tap. Many in Africa must depend on a distant river for water of uncertain quality.

Great Britain gives good illustration of uneven distribution. The lowlands of the east and south have relatively low rainfall totals, and high losses through evaporation and transpiration (together known as *evapotranspiration*). In these lowlands, households and factories combine to create a high demand for water. Supplies are taken from rivers and from wells drilled into aquifers. London, for instance, takes water from Thames and Chalk. However, over lowland areas generally, supplies are inadequate.

In contrast, the thinly-peopled upland areas to the west of Britain, with high precipitation and low evapotranspiration, have water in abundance. Demand is small and some of the surplus is transferred to meet the needs of populous lowland centres such as Liverpool (Fig. 38).

The demand for water in lowland Britain continues to grow. Population growth and a higher standard of living give rise to more water-consuming devices such as washing-machines and dishwashers. Industry retains its thirst, and in agriculture, especially towards the drier east of the country, summer irrigation becomes more popular.

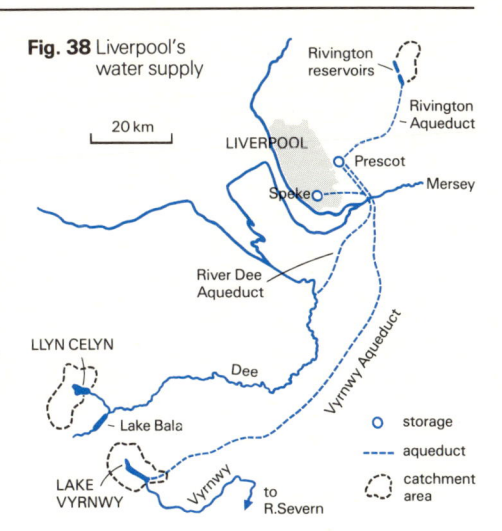

Fig. 38 Liverpool's water supply

Conflicts of Interest

To satisfy increased demand, one proposal is new reservoirs in upland areas. This does not meet with universal approval. Among the likely list of objectors are:
- upland sheep farmers who will lose their livelihood as essential valley land is submerged;
- walkers who regret the loss of cross-valley path and track;
- conservationists who feel that a large concrete dam will destroy for ever the natural beauty of an upland valley, which may, like many reservoir sites, lie within a National Park;
- naturalists who will be sad at the loss of wildlife habitats.

A second proposal is to build barrages across major estuaries such as those of Morecambe Bay and the River Dee. The arguments that must be carefully balanced before a decision is taken are summarised below:

FOR

1. Creation of large freshwater reservoir.

2. Recreational opportunities for water sports.

3. Road along top of barrage might improve local communications.

4. Possible inclusion of hydro-electric power scheme.

5. Stimulus to industry and creation of jobs.

AGAINST

1. High cost. Vast amount of money involved could be more usefully spent on other projects.

2. Loss of land and landscapes.

3. Destruction of salt-marsh – important wildlife habitat.

4. Possible interruption of navigation.

5. Danger of pollution from inflowing rivers.

Water Pollution

The purity of the water in many of the world's rivers has been destroyed by pollution, the main sources of which are:
- sewage, which prompts health risks in many Third World countries, where the river may also serve as water supply.
- factories which make or use chemicals and often dispose of surplus materials into rivers. This waste may be toxic to life in the river.
- modern intensive-farming methods. Chemical fertilisers may be washed through the soil and into the rivers. Excess animal manure, especially the slurry from pig-farming, can have a similar destination. The consequence is an increase of nitrates and phosphates in the water. Algae thrive in the enriched waters and deprive other forms of life of essential oxygen. Food-chains are broken and life in and above river and lake is depleted or destroyed. The lack of wildlife and the green bloom of algae are consequences that may greatly damage a river's amenity value;
- unauthorised dumping. An inconsiderate public sometimes sees rivers as free disposal systems for rubbish.

Polluted rivers naturally pollute the seas into which they flow. Marine pollution is increased by:
- the piping out to sea of untreated sewage;
- slightly radioactive liquid waste from coastal nuclear power-stations;
- oil discharged from tankers, which may be simple spillage, the result of a tanker flushing its tanks at sea, or in some cases massive oil-slicks if a tanker is holed or sinks.

Pollution is worst in small, enclosed areas where input is high. The North Sea is one example which currently gives great cause for concern.

Points to Note

1. Ensure that you know the meaning of the technical terms introduced in the early part of this chapter – infiltration, through-flow, etc. Consolidate by preparing simple but accurate definitions.

2. Know, too, the methods employed to obtain supplies of water and the contrasts between advanced and developing countries. One method that might be overlooked is *desalination*. This is the production of fresh water from sea water. It is a costly process in terms of energy, and so its use is largely restricted to the oil-rich desert states of the Persian Gulf.

3. Note examples of the influence on people of the topics considered in this chapter – variations in river discharge, for example. Flooding has a clear set of consequences, but low levels of discharge can also be significant – for navigation, for industry, and in many parts of the world, for domestic water supply.

4. The GCSE National Criteria for Geography aim to encourage an appreciation of *values*. It is hoped that students will come to appreciate the differing attitudes that people may have about a current issue of geographical interest, and how these attitudes may influence the making of decisions. A proposed new upland reservoir is a typical topic. Think about it. Debate it with yourself, playing all the parts. *Evaluate* the advantages and disadvantages of the proposed scheme. Try to come to a balanced judgement, for or against.

In similar fashion, consideration of a proposal to build a barrage across an estuary will be worthwhile.

5. Pollution of rivers and seas is linked to that of the atmosphere to form a major issue of current concern, and hence of examination significance.

5 Landscapes

A variety of natural processes act upon the rocks of the Earth's crust to create the great diversity of scenery that we see about us.

Weathering

Weathering is the decay and breakdown of rock simply through exposure to the atmosphere. Many separate processes make a contribution to weathering, which will, in time, cause the disintegration of even the toughest rock. *Freeze-thaw* is an example of a *physical* weathering process. Water occupying the cracks and pores in a rock will expand on freezing. Expansion exerts pressure on the rock, which is released with the thaw. Frequent repetition of this freeze-thaw cycle can, in time, cause the rock to crack and particles to fall away.

Carbonation is one of many forms of *chemical* weathering. Rain combines with carbon dioxide in the atmosphere to become weak carbonic acid. This turns calcium carbonate in the rock into soluble calcium bicarbonate which is then removed in solution.

Vegetation makes a contribution to weathering through the expansion of roots in rock crevices, but, more significantly, by the addition, through decay, of destructive acids.

The weathering of rock produces *regolith*, which with the addition of organic matter becomes soil.

The products of the weathering processes on a level rock surface remain in place, to become in time a thick layer of fine particles. On slopes, however, gravity powers the downslope movement of weathered material.

Mass Movement

This is the collective name given to the many processes by which weathered rock particles move downslope under the influence of gravity. Two contrasting types of mass movement, rapid and slow, respectively, are illustrated in Fig. 39 and Fig. 40.

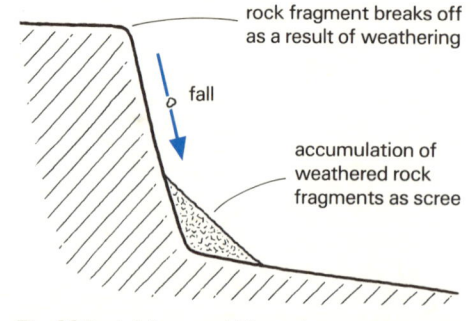

Fig. 39 Rock fall — a rapid form of mass movement

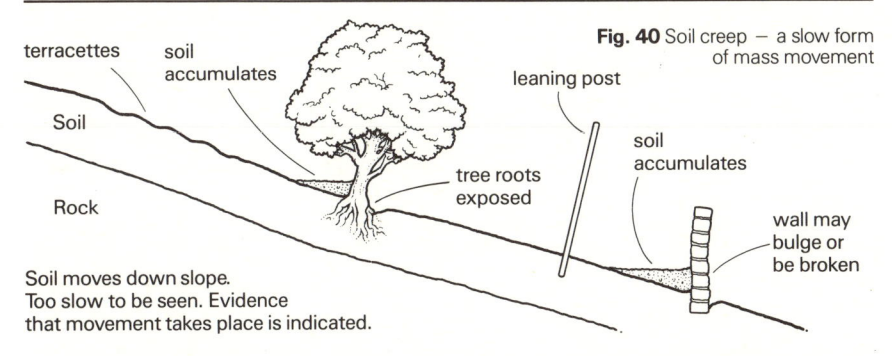

The Work of Rivers · Transportation

Fig. 40 Soil creep — a slow form of mass movement

terracettes
soil accumulates
Soil
Rock
leaning post
tree roots exposed
soil accumulates
wall may bulge or be broken

Soil moves down slope. Too slow to be seen. Evidence that movement takes place is indicated.

Mass movement is generally slight, slow and inoffensive, but in rare and extreme circumstances it can become a natural hazard. Whole hillsides may collapse, bringing death and destruction to the valley below. Such happenings are most likely to occur on steep, high slopes where a weak, permeable rock rests upon steeply-dipping impermeable layers. Heavy rain saturates, and so increases the weight of, the surface rocks, which slide down over the water-lubricated junction with the impermeable rock. The resultant landslide may carry away all in its path. Material can temporarily dam a river and serious floods may occur when the river breaks through the new weak barrier.

The Work of Rivers

Rivers play the major role in landscape creation. They work in several ways.

Transportation

Rivers transport a load of rock material. The load is moved in suspension, in solution, and by being forced to 'jump' or roll along the bed of the river channel. A river's ability to transport depends on volume and velocity (speed). The bigger the river and the faster it flows, the more it can carry.

Fig. 41 emphasises the important point that the various processes of landscape formation work hand in hand. It shows how weathering, mass movement and river transport combine to lower the valley sides and hence the land surface.

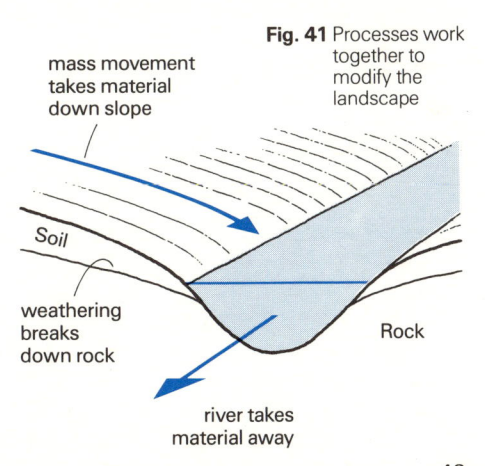

Fig. 41 Processes work together to modify the landscape

mass movement takes material down slope
Soil
weathering breaks down rock
Rock
river takes material away

43

Erosion · Deposition

Erosion

a) *downward erosion*
   Thanks to the impact of flowing water, solution, and the abrasive effect of its solid load, the river wears away the rock over which it flows. Slowly the bed of the river is lowered.

b) *lateral erosion*
   Fig. 42 shows that on the outside of a bend the river erodes and undercuts the bank, which causes it to collapse into the river to be transported away. The process of undercutting and collapse, often repeated, leads to a lateral (sideways) movement of the side of the channel.

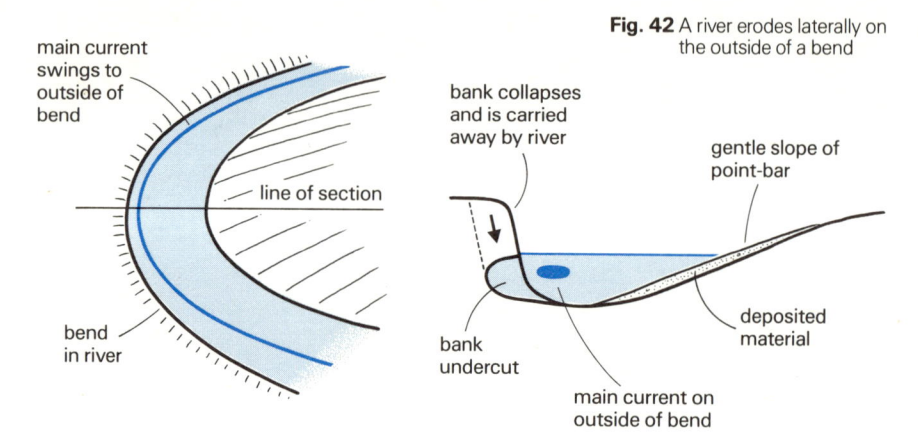

Fig. 42 A river erodes laterally on the outside of a bend

Deposition

When the velocity of a river is reduced, its ability to transport is also reduced, and part of its load may be deposited. This happens noticeably when a well-loaded river flows into the quiet waters of a lake, which in time will be removed from the landscape as it becomes filled with deposited material.

Fig. 42 contains another example. In the shallow waters of the inside of the bend, the speed of flow is low, so deposition takes place. Incidentally, this deposition keeps pace with lateral erosion, so the channel, though shifting, does not get any wider.

River Landforms

Erosion and deposition play major roles in the formation of the familiar landforms associated with the course of a river valley.

Valley Cross-Section

This represents a balance between the effect of deepening and widening processes. Examples are shown in Fig. 43.

River Landforms

Fig. 43 Contrasts in a valley cross-section

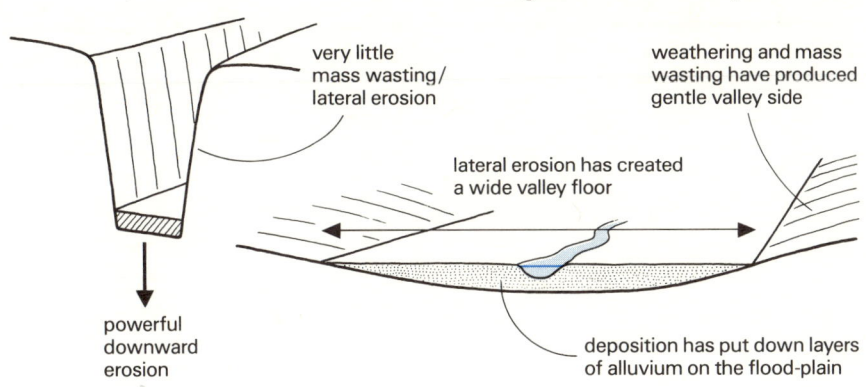

- very little mass wasting/lateral erosion
- powerful downward erosion
- weathering and mass wasting have produced gentle valley side
- lateral erosion has created a wide valley floor
- deposition has put down layers of alluvium on the flood-plain

Waterfalls

Many waterfalls are created by the river itself, and Fig. 44 illustrates how. This is a good example of how relative rock resistance can influence landscape formation. Note that not all waterfalls are created by rivers. Earth movements, and especially the work of ice, may lead to the formation of many waterfalls.

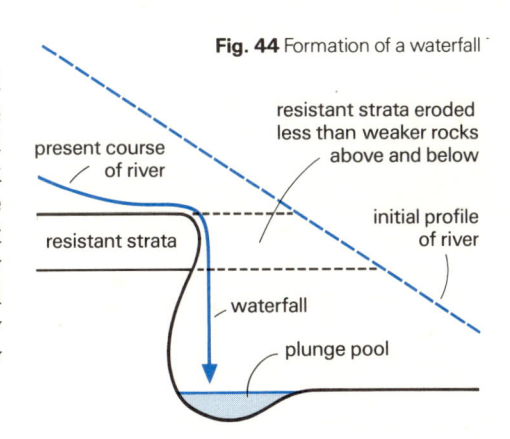

Fig. 44 Formation of a waterfall

- present course of river
- resistant strata
- resistant strata eroded less than weaker rocks above and below
- initial profile of river
- waterfall
- plunge pool

Ox-Bow Lake

Fig. 45 shows that this distinctive feature of the flood-plains of large rivers is due to lateral erosion and deposition.

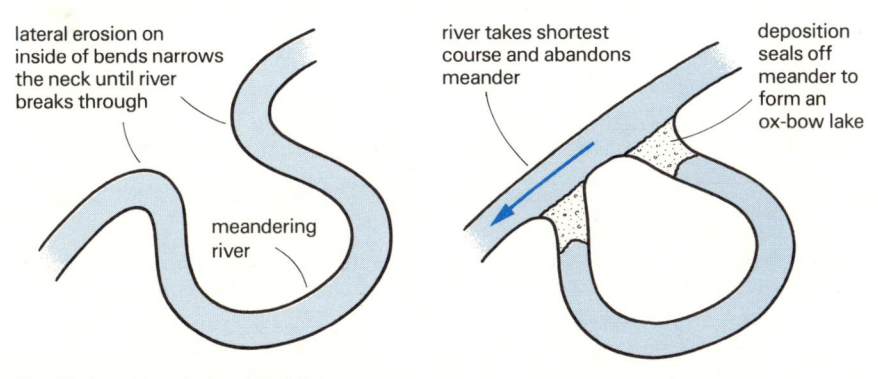

- lateral erosion on inside of bends narrows the neck until river breaks through
- meandering river
- river takes shortest course and abandons meander
- deposition seals off meander to form an ox-bow lake

Fig. 45 Formation of an ox-bow lake

45

Lakes

Lakes can be formed in a variety of ways. Earth movements and the work of ice are responsible for many. Fig. 46 shows that lakes are temporary features.

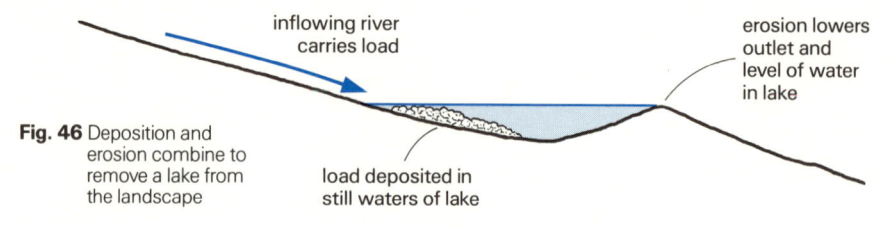

Fig. 46 Deposition and erosion combine to remove a lake from the landscape

Deltas

When a river meets the sea, its speed is rapidly checked and deposition takes place. It silts up estuaries, or, if it flows into the open sea, it may create a *delta* (Fig. 47). Deltas are common in quiet sea areas such as the Mediterranean, where major rivers, e.g. the Nile and Rhône, carry large loads. Deposition extends the river as a large area of new flat land is created. Land is so flat that river channels frequently split up into *distributaries*. Flooding is frequent, and often hazardous to the farming populations attracted by the richness of the fertile alluvial soil.

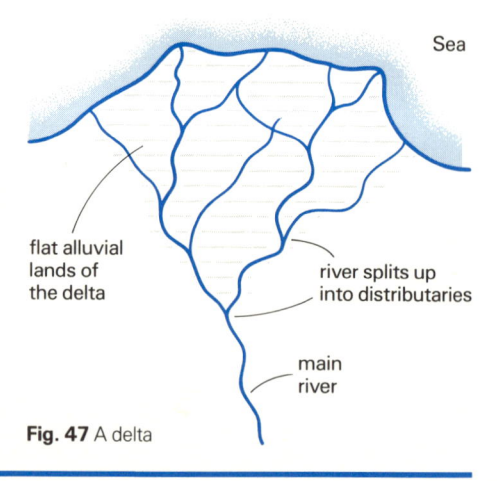

Fig. 47 A delta

The Work of Ice

Moving ice, like flowing water, erodes, transports and deposits. The effects of ice are still sharp and fresh on the landscapes of such upland areas as the Lake District, North Wales, and the Highlands of Scotland. Two sets of distinctive upland landforms may be recognised.

1. **Cirques (Corries), Arêtes and Pyramidal Peaks**

The story of the formation of a cirque starts at the onset of the ice age with the accumulation of snow in a sheltered hollow, especially if facing north, in an upland mass. Snow and its melt-waters encourage weathering, and the hollow is enlarged. In time it becomes large enough to support a small glacier. This mass of ice, formed by the compaction of snow, moves slowly out of the hollow, further enlarging it on the way.

The glacier erodes in two ways:
- *plucking* – ice freezes on to weathered and weakened rock and blocks are quarried away when the glacier moves on;
- *abrasion* – rocks embedded in the base of the glacier scratch and grind away at the rock, the surface of which is steadily lowered.

The hollow is deepened and enlarged into the dramatic landscape feature known as a *cirque* or *corrie*. It has three high and precipitous sides and a floor often slightly hollowed by abrasion, which now holds a small lake or tarn. Fig. 48 shows a cirque in a cross-section.

Fig. 48 Cross-section of a cirque (corrie or cwm)

- pre-glacial landscape
- small streams flow out to join river in major valley
- back wall made steep and high by plucking
- tarn
- abrasion lowered and hollowed the floor

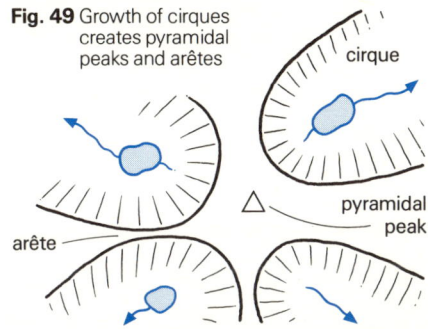

Fig. 49 Growth of cirques creates pyramidal peaks and arêtes

- cirque
- arête
- pyramidal peak

When an upland mass supports a number of cirques, the growth of each takes its steep walls closer to those of a neighbour. In time, the land between two cirques may be reduced to a dramatic, knife-edged ridge known as an *arête* (Fig. 49). The high meeting-point of several arêtes is a *pyramidal peak*. Famous British summits such as Snowdon and Helvellyn, which rise above upland plateaus, well illustrate these distinctive and attractive landform features.

2. Glacial Troughs

During the ice age, small glaciers from many cirques contributed to major glaciers which took over the valleys of upland areas, and by powerful downward erosion brought about great changes to the landscape. Examination of Fig. 50 reveals that the pre-glacial valley was greatly overdeepened by ice erosion. Note that the upper valley sides were hardly touched by ice. These gentle pre-glacial slopes can be recognised today, especially in high mountains such as the Alps – where they are confusingly known as alps!

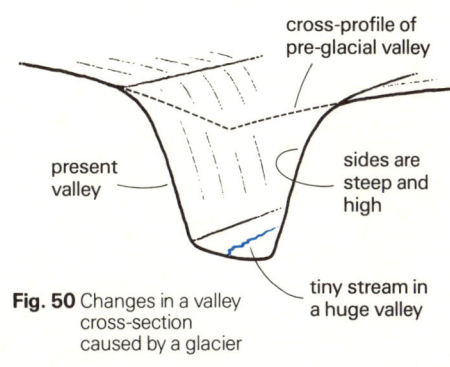

Fig. 50 Changes in a valley cross-section caused by a glacier

- cross-profile of pre-glacial valley
- present valley
- sides are steep and high
- tiny stream in a huge valley

Glacial Troughs · Landforms Due to Deposition

A glacier is obviously much less flexible than running water. It cannot adapt to the twists and turns of a normal river valley (Fig. 51). It rides roughshod over the lower ends of the spurs and grinds them away (Fig. 52). Thus the glacial trough is straight and the blunted ends of the spurs can often be identified in the steep, high valley walls (truncated spurs).

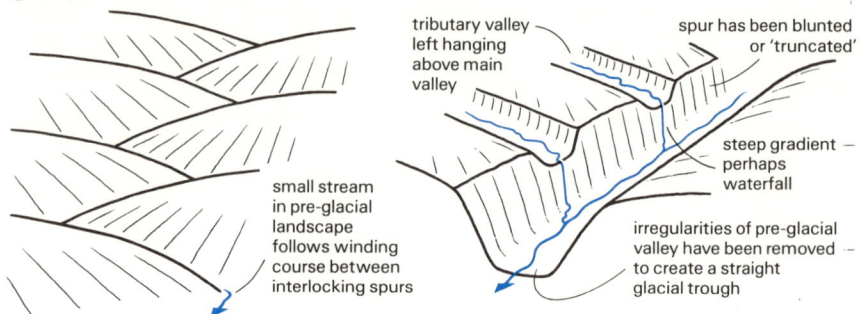

Fig. 51 A river valley

Fig. 52 Features of a glacial trough

Note, too, from Fig. 52, how tributary valleys which held only small glaciers during the ice age were deepened less, and today 'hang' over their main valley. These tributary valleys are now known, naturally, as *hanging valleys*.

Glacial troughs often include long, relatively narrow lakes, known from their shape as *ribbon lakes*. They represent overdeepening of the valley floor, due, perhaps, to the presence of softer or weaker rock, or locally more effective erosion.

Landforms Due to Deposition

Deposition by ice has widespread and significant impact on the landscape. Its impact is greatest in lowland areas dominated not by glaciers, but by massive ice-sheets such as those which, at intervals during the ice age, covered lowland Britain as far south as the line of the river Thames. Fig. 53 accounts for the formation of *terminal moraine* and *outwash plain*.

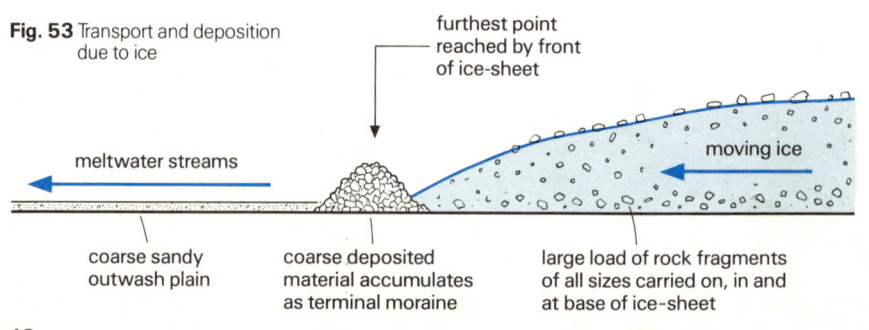

Fig. 53 Transport and deposition due to ice

When, with the ending of the ice age, the ice-sheet wasted away, its load of unsorted material was spread on the surface as *boulder clay*. This mixed deposit of the finest clays, studded with sub-angular boulders of all sizes, blankets the post-glacial landscapes to great depths. Sometimes it is spread more or less evenly, but in some areas it has been hummocked up into a swarm of low, streamlined hills known as *drumlins*, to give the low but distinctive landscape suggested by Fig. 54.

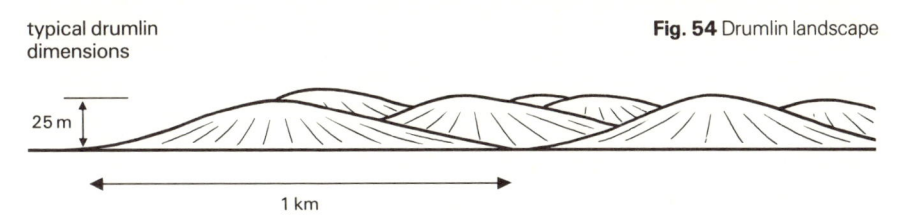

typical drumlin dimensions

Fig. 54 Drumlin landscape

25 m

1 km

The Work of the Sea

The sea, like the other agents of erosion, erodes, transports and deposits. It does so through the power of its waves. These are caused by the friction of wind on the water surface. The stronger the wind, and the further it has travelled over the open sea (the *fetch*), the more powerful the wave. The erosive effect of wave action is seen in the following common coastal features.

Headlands and Bays

Waves may effectively scoop out areas of weaker rocks to form bays. Tougher rocks stand out as headlands, as in the Swanage area of Dorset (Fig. 55). Note that the largest bays are not caused by erosion, but by earth movements or by rises in the level of the sea.

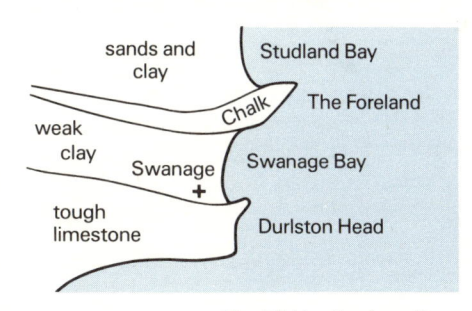

Fig. 55 Headlands and bays

Cliffs

Fig. 56 indicates that wave action is concentrated in the narrow zone between high-tide and low-tide levels. Waves erode a notch, the land above collapses, and a new cliff is born. As soon as the collapsed material has been removed, undercutting can begin again. Repetition of the cycle of undercutting, collapse and removal leads to the retreat of the cliffs, and the creation of a wave-cut platform of flat rock, often covered by a layer of sand and shingle. As the wave-cut platform becomes wider, the energy of the incoming waves is reduced, and hence, their ability to erode the land is also reduced.

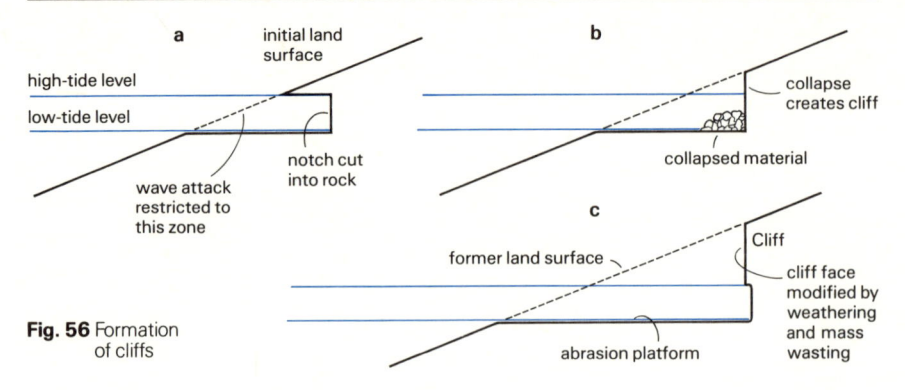

Cliff Scenery

Fig. 56 Formation of cliffs

(a) initial land surface; high-tide level; low-tide level; wave attack restricted to this zone; notch cut into rock

(b) collapse creates cliff; collapsed material

(c) former land surface; Cliff; cliff face modified by weathering and mass wasting; abrasion platform

Cliff Scenery

Waves are highly selective in their erosive work. On a cliffed coastline they pick out the slightest weaknesses, such as a fault or a much-jointed section of rock, to carve the intricate details of cliff scenery. Fig. 57 explains the formation of caves and natural arches. Should the arch collapse, a large rock is left upstanding in the sea. This is known as a *stack* – the name given to any isolated rock that is left behind as the cliff retreats.

Fig. 57 Features of cliff scenery

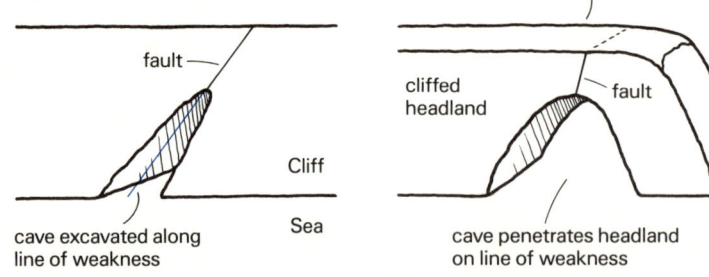

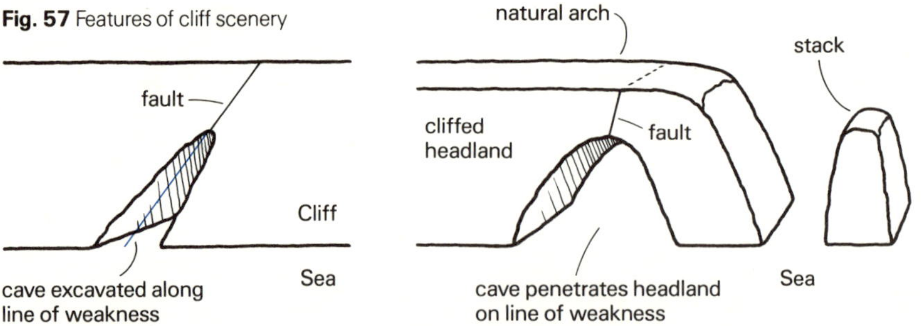

fault; Cliff; Sea; cave excavated along line of weakness

natural arch; stack; cliffed headland; fault; Sea; cave penetrates headland on line of weakness

Constructive Work of the Sea

Breaking waves can transport beach material along the shore. The process is known as *longshore drift*, and may be understood with the help of Fig. 58. Here, it is assumed that the most frequent and/or most powerful waves arrive from the south-west. The waves break on the shore obliquely. Beach material – a pebble (P) – will

Fig. 58 Longshore drift

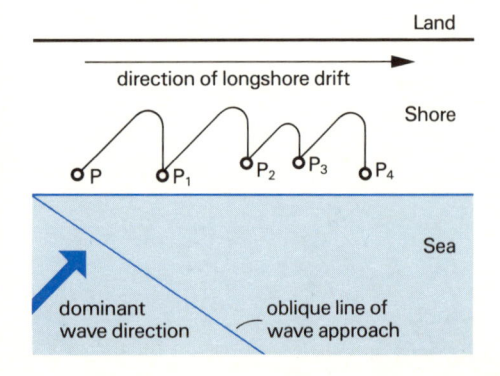

Land; direction of longshore drift; Shore; P, P_1, P_2, P_3, P_4; Sea; dominant wave direction; oblique line of wave approach

be driven obliquely up the shelving shore, but when the power of the breaking wave (*swash*) is spent, the backwash takes the pebble down the shore at right angles, to a new position (P_1). The pebble has been shifted slightly to the right. This, frequently but irregularly repeated, leads to a significant drift of material along the shore. When the direction of the coast changes, the longshore drift may persist to create small but interesting features of coastal scenery. A long, narrow, often hooked, projection of beach material into a bay or an estuary is known as a *spit*, such as Spurn Head at the mouth of the Humber. Small, quiet bays may be sealed off completely by a *bar*. Should longshore drift cause an island to be linked to the mainland, a *tombolo* is the result.

Groynes are stout barriers erected across the shore at right angles to the land. They are designed to reduce the loss of beach material by longshore drift. This they do at the cost of the distortion of shape indicated in Fig. 59.

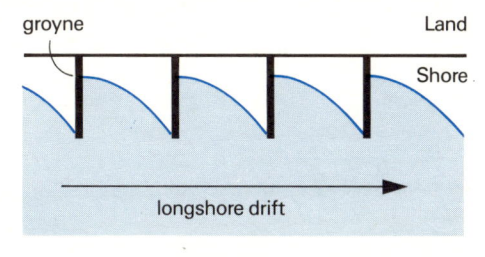

Fig. 59 The effect of groynes on the shape of a beach

Sea-Level Changes

The level of contact between land and sea is mean sea-level. But this can change.

1. Movements within the Earth's crust may locally raise or lower the land relative to the sea.
2. Changes in world climate can increase or reduce the amount of ice in the system (Fig. 32, page 35). This leads to change in the amount of water in the seas and hence its level.

Changes in mean sea-level have a significant effect on the form of the coast. Consider the river sketched in Fig. 60. Imagine that mean sea-level slowly rises by 20 m. The former valley is now a winding, many-branched estuary. This type of estuary, common in Devon and Cornwall, is known as a *ria*.

Should a rising sea-level submerge the lower levels of a glacial trough, a *fiord* is the result.

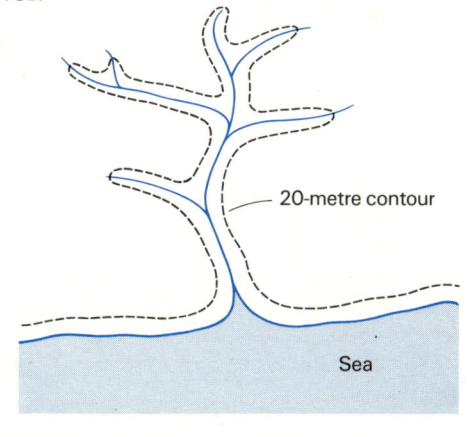

Fig. 60 Formation of ria

51

Limestone Landscapes

The character of some landscapes is profoundly influenced by the nature of the rock on which the natural processes work. Limestone is a prime example. This pale, tough rock can be removed in solution and carries a rectilinear pattern of well-marked joints and bedding planes. Solution is greatest along these lines of weakness, and distinctive scenery is created.

Fig. 61 Limestone pavement

clints — joints enlarged by solution into deep narrow grikes which divide the rock into clints

Limestone Pavement

Limestone pavement is a distinctive feature. It is found typically in upland outcrops of level strata – the Yorkshire Dales, for instance. Fig. 61 explains its formation.

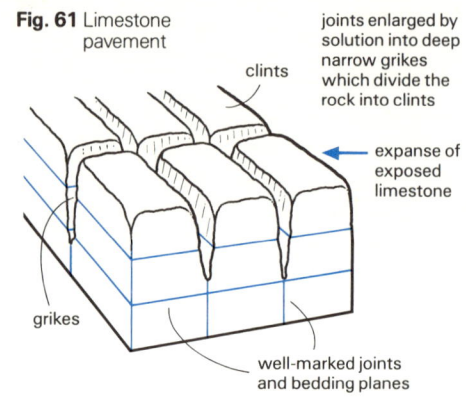

expanse of exposed limestone

grikes

well-marked joints and bedding planes

Underground Drainage

Look at Fig. 62. A stream rising on impermeable rock flows on to the limestone. Water seeps down joints which are enlarged by solution. Eventually the stream can disappear down the first of these enlarged joints which are known as *swallow-* (or *pot-*) *holes*. The former course of the stream over the limestone is now a dry valley. Solution and river erosion are effective underground, and the limestone is dissolved and carved into complex systems of channels, caves, and caverns. The underground river emerges as a powerful spring where the limestone rests on impermeable rock.

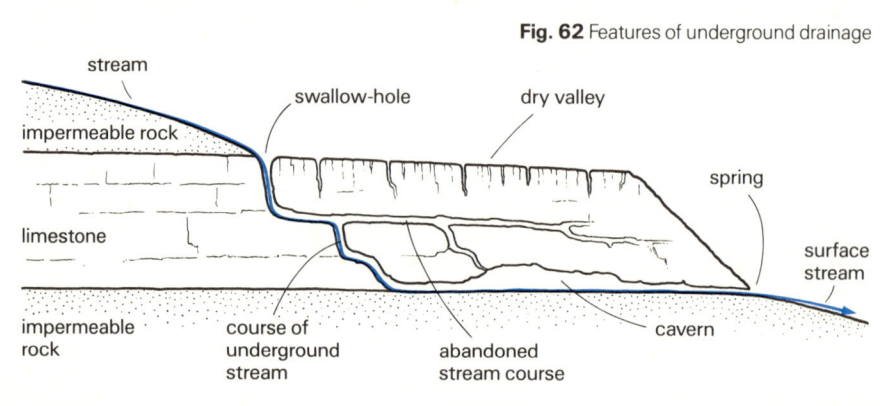

Fig. 62 Features of underground drainage

stream / impermeable rock / swallow-hole / dry valley / spring / limestone / surface stream / impermeable rock / course of underground stream / abandoned stream course / cavern

Points to Note

1. Be prepared to describe and explain the formation of individual landforms. To prepare for description, make sure you have a clear picture in your mind of what they look like. This can be greatly aided by the study of photographs. Make sure you are familiar with the patterns the different landforms make in the contours of the OS maps.

The key to explanation is process. If you understand the process of longshore drift, for instance, explanation of spits will easily follow. Oxbow lakes, for example, are appreciated as the result of both lateral erosion and deposition.

Remember, too, the important role played by the relative resistance of rock in the detail of scenery and landform.

2. Please pay attention to the diagrams. They do more than keep sections of the text apart. They are an aid to understanding and an acceptable form of answer to many questions. Indeed, examiners may thoughtfully provide you with an appropriate space to fill. The diagrams have been kept simple. Don't just give them a passing glance – study them. Look at each carefully and patiently and let their image be recorded in your memory. Test yourself by reproducing them from memory – not forgetting the essential labelling.

3. Landscapes obviously have a great influence on human activities, and these links are often the target for exam questions. So bear this in mind as you make your way through subsequent chapters. These links are the best source of required examples. If, for instance, the Lake District is the National Park you have chosen for study, the examples of Red Tarn (cirque), Striding Edge (arête) and Helvellyn(pyramidal peak) will be doubly useful.

4. Information on lakes may profitably be gathered together into a useful little study. Include formation, removal, and human significance.

Types of Farming

6 Agriculture

Agriculture is a *primary* economic activity – it is concerned with the exploitation of natural resources. It shares this classification with activities such as mining, fishing and lumbering. These are distinguished from *secondary* activities, i.e. manufacturing industry, and *tertiary* ones, which are concerned with the provision of services.

It is important to be clear about the meaning of the terms used to identify the different types of farm and farm economy.

Arable. The growing of crops. These are described as 'cash' if sold, and 'fodder' if retained on the farm for animals.

Pastoral. The keeping of livestock.

Mixed. The combination of growing crops and rearing livestock in one enterprise.

Commercial. Farm produce is sold. The farmer generally aims to make maximum profit from the land (while maintaining or improving its quality). Profit is the income from the sale of crops and livestock, less the costs of production.

Subsistence. Farm output is used to sustain the farmer and his family, but there is no surplus production to be sold.

Intensive. Much labour and/or capital is devoted – usually to a relatively small area – to achieve a high yield per hectare.

Extensive. Large landholdings receive relatively little labour or capital. Output per hectare is low.

Thus, cattle ranching can be described as extensive commercial pastoralism. Market gardening, in contrast, is an example of an intensive commercial arable enterprise.

Further detail may be added by consideration of location and tenure.

Location. This may be *sedentary* (fixed) or *shifting* (subject to change). Most enterprises are sedentary, but shifting cultivation and pastoral nomadism are exceptions.

Land tenure (i.e. occupation). There are four common types of tenure:

i) *Owner-occupation.* The land is worked by the landowner.
ii) *Rented.* The farmer pays rent to the landowner for use of the land. In many parts of the Third World, rent is paid not in money but in a share (perhaps as much as a half or two-thirds) of the crop. This is *share-cropping*.
iii) *Collective.* The land is owned collectively by a group.
iv) *State ownership.* The land is owned by the state as in the centrally-planned (communist) countries.

The Farmer's Choice

The way in which any piece of land is used is the result of a deliberate decision. There are many factors which influence land-use decisions. The farmer wishing to make best use of his land must consider and evaluate the influences indicated in Fig. 63 before making up his mind. His task is hard because the labels in the diagram represent not single factors but groups. Illustration with familiar examples is given below.

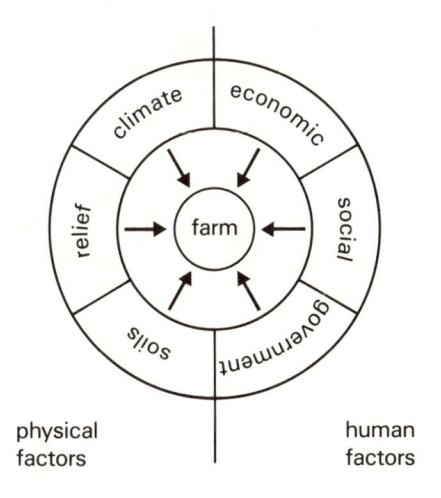

Fig. 63 Factors influencing the farmer's choice of land use

Physical Factors

- **Climate**, in its control of temperature and moisture, clearly has a major influence on the choice of farm enterprise. In England, for instance, the warmer, drier east is favoured for cereals, whereas the wetter west is better suited to grass/pasture. Farmers in the Canadian Prairies find that a growing season of approximately 100 days will cater for the needs of wheat but not of maize. A choice of orchard crops may be rejected on a particular farm because of the risk of a late killing frost.
- **Soil** shows variation in, among other things, depth, fertility and drainage, all of which may influence the farmer's choice. Thin soils, as on chalk, are better suited to cereals than to root crops. Heavy clay soils, moist and hard to plough, are often left in pasture.
- **Relief** is another important physical factor. Land sloping at more than 11° is difficult to plough, and is usually given over to pasture. Flat land poses problems of drainage, and hence flood-plains may be used for rich hay meadows.

Relief influences agriculture most profoundly through its modification of climate. In temperate latitudes, increased altitude is marked by lower temperatures, a shorter growing season and increased rainfall, which together progressively reduce agricultural opportunities. Tropical mountains offer a variety of climates which are reflected in the crops grown. In South America, cacao and bananas may flourish in the hot, wet conditions at sea-level. Coffee and maize take over in the sub-tropical conditions at higher altitude, to be replaced in their turn by temperate crops such as barley and potatoes. Near the summit, grazing of scanty natural pasture is the only opportunity.

Human Factors

- **Market.** The commercial farmer is obviously influenced in decision-making by the size of the market and the prices that prevail for a product. Low prices naturally discourage production. Co-operative marketing is increasing in importance in many parts of the world. In Denmark, for instance, a large number of small, independent farmers band together to establish, say, a co-operative creamery, which takes all milk output, processes it, and markets the butter, cheese, etc. Creamery profits are shared among the farmers.

  In Denmark, co-operation is successfully applied to all manner of farm inputs and outputs. It enables small farmers to compete successfully.

- **Transport.** The farmer must be able to call upon efficient transport if he is to deliver his produce to market, and lack of such transport facilities is often a handicap in the Third World. In advanced countries, the cost and speed of transport can be important. The production of crops which bear high transport charges is encouraged near the market. Peas, for example, must be delivered to the freezing factory within an hour and a half of picking.

- **Labour Costs.** High labour costs encourage mechanisation, and arable farming at the expense of pastoral.

- **Capital** is money available for investment. Its availability has a great influence on the level of technology in use – whether, for instance, it is that of the hoe or the tractor. Where capital is abundant and available at relatively low cost (interest), physical controls on agriculture may be modified, e.g. wetlands may be drained for arable crops; and, in glasshouses, climate can be created to order.

- **Farm Size.** Small farms must be worked intensively to yield a satisfactory profit. Only large farms can profit fully from mechanisation.

- **Government Influence** is obviously important in centrally-planned (communist) economies. On the collective farms (kolkhozi) of the USSR the land is owned by the state, which makes major decisions and sets production targets; but the land is worked collectively under the guidance of an elected committee.

  Elsewhere, many governments attempt to influence the type and/or amount of production by price support, direct support or taxation incentives.

The Farm as a System

The farm economy can often be better understood if studied as a system. The flow diagram (Fig. 64) gives a general picture. The square box encloses buildings, land and processes. Activity depends upon a

Extensive Cereal Cultivation

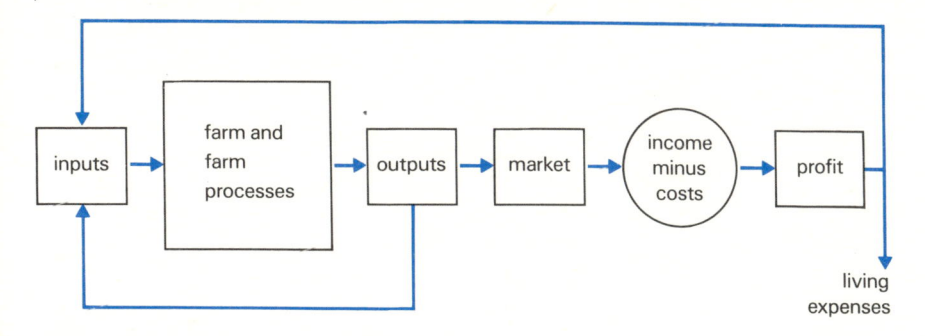

Fig. 64 System diagram – commercial farming

range of inputs, important examples of which are labour, energy, seeds, fertilisers. Some farm output – fodder, for example – may be an input for the feeding of livestock, but the bulk – cash crops and/or animals – is destined for the market. This is the *point of sale*. It may be a local town, a supermarket chain or a processing factory. At the end of the flow, the farmer must divide his profits between living expenses and the cost of next year's inputs.

Specific Examples of Farming
Extensive Cereal Cultivation

Some of the considerations that influence the farmer's choice in the southern prairies of Canada may be appreciated from Fig. 26 (page 28).
- There is a growing season of 100 days or more.
- The summer maximum of rain normally ensures adequate soil moisture.
- There are warm, sunny summers.

Other physical factors include:
- The soil is deep and fertile.
- The level prairie relief permits economic use of large machines.

Additional factors are:
- large landholdings in owner occupation;
- capital widely available;
- efficient transport;
- world market;
- government support.

Against these favourable factors must be set the occasional risk of natural hazards such as drought, hailstorms and plant disease which may reduce the harvest.

The cultivation of cereals, especially wheat, is the most profitable land use, and hence the farmer's choice.

57

Hill Sheep-Farming

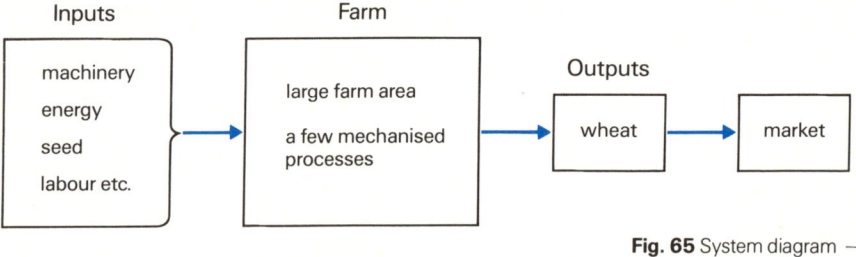

Fig. 65 System diagram — commercial wheat farming

Inputs: machinery, energy, seed, labour etc.

Farm: large farm area, a few mechanised processes

Outputs: wheat → market

As the flow diagram (Fig. 65) suggests, it is a relatively simple agricultural system. Farm processes are limited to spring ploughing, preparation, drilling and autumn harvest. Total inputs, relative to farm area, are small. Most significant is the large investment in massive machines which make it possible to cultivate huge areas with a small labour force. Output per hectare is generally low, but output per man is high. There is a large surplus available for domestic and world markets. This farming enterprise may be classified as *extensive commercial arable*.

Hill Sheep-Farming

This is typical of Britain's wet and westerly uplands such as North Wales and the Highlands of Scotland. Fig. 66 shows a simple pattern of land use that is greatly influenced by the factor of relief. Farm buildings are sited on the floor of a glacial trough, but by far the greater part of the farm area lies on steep, high valley sides and the plateau above. Here, slopes are too steep to plough, carry thin, acid, infertile soil, and suffer a climate that deteriorates with altitude. All these factors combine to make cultivation impossible. The land supports poor-quality grazing.

In contrast, the small patch of level valley floor included within the farm has deeper soils of modest fertility and is cultivable. The moist, mild, cloudy climate of western Britain favours grass and fodder rather than cash crops. In this environment, the farmer does not have much choice. The rearing of sheep is the only practical agricultural use of the land.

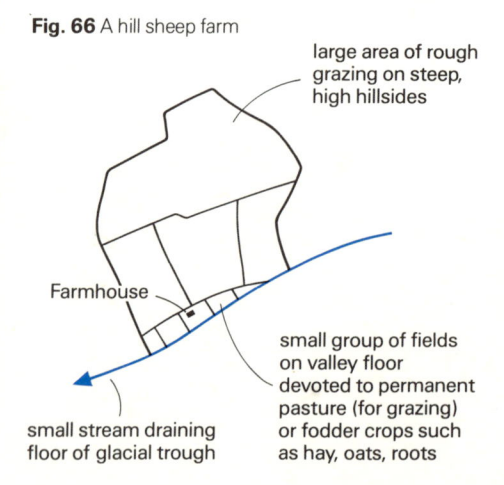

Fig. 66 A hill sheep farm

- large area of rough grazing on steep, high hillsides
- Farmhouse
- small group of fields on valley floor devoted to permanent pasture (for grazing) or fodder crops such as hay, oats, roots
- small stream draining floor of glacial trough

Mixed Farming

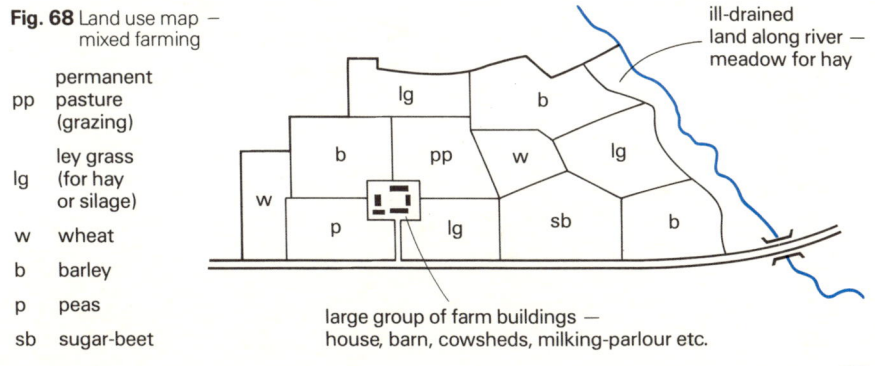

Fig. 67 System diagram – hill sheep farming

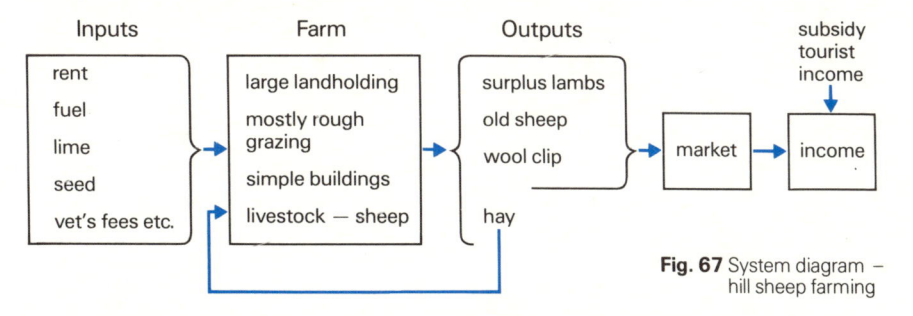

Inputs	Farm	Outputs	
rent	large landholding	surplus lambs	subsidy tourist income
fuel	mostly rough grazing	old sheep	
lime		wool clip	→ market → income
seed	simple buildings		
vet's fees etc.	livestock — sheep	hay	

This type of farm economy demands the close integration of the two contrasting types of land – upland and lowland. Sheep spend most of the year on the rough pasture of the hillsides, but the lowland is vital for grazing and supplementary feed at such times as lambing, and during harsh winter weather.

As suggested in Fig. 67, this is a relatively simple farm economy. Only small amounts of inputs are required. The value of the outputs tends to be low — often only slightly more than the cost of the inputs. Profits are not high. This type of farming is therefore described as *marginal*. Often, it is only made possible by subsidy and/or income from the tourist industry. If the farmer has sufficient valley land, the rearing of a few cattle may provide a small additional income. Hill sheep-farming is classified as *extensive commercial pastoral*.

Mixed Farming

Land use typical of *intensive commercial mixed* farming is illustrated by Fig. 68. A variety of crops is grown – all chosen with due regard to the farm's environment. They yield well in the temperate climate, deep fertile soils, and gentle relief of much of eastern England. Most are cash crops, sold at market, or, in the case of sugar-beet and peas, direct to local factories. Permanent pasture provides grazing, and ley grass and meadow yield grass for hay or silage, essential for winter feeding of a herd of dairy or beef cattle.

Fig. 68 Land use map – mixed farming

- pp permanent pasture (grazing)
- lg ley grass (for hay or silage)
- w wheat
- b barley
- p peas
- sb sugar-beet

ill-drained land along river — meadow for hay

large group of farm buildings — house, barn, cowsheds, milking-parlour etc.

Intensive Rice-Farming

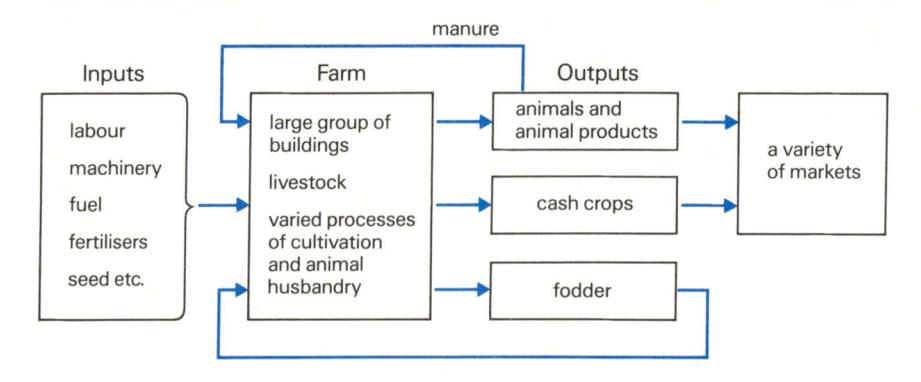

Fig. 69 System diagram – mixed farming

The farm system is illustrated in Fig. 69. The complexity of the enterprise has advantages.
1. Cultivation of a range of crops:
   a) demands labour at different times – a variety of different crops spreads the farm work-load more evenly;
   b) limits possible damage by inclement weather, disease, and insect pests, hazards which affect only individual crops and activities;
   c) permits beneficial crop rotations. Thus the growth of peas adds nitrogen to the soil; this benefits the cereal crops which follow in the same field.
2. The inclusion of livestock in the system:
   a) ensures that the 'waste' from cash crops, such as sugar-beet tops and pea vines, can make good fodder.
   b) utilises straw as bedding for animals. With natural additions, the rotted mixture is a fine manure which increases fertility and the organic content of the soil.

Intensive Rice-Farming

Tropical environments also prompt a varied agricultural response.

The flood-plains and deltas in areas of monsoon climate (Fig. 25, page 28) provide a favourable agricultural environment. The combined delta of the rivers Ganges and Brahmaputra, shared by India and Bangladesh, is an example. The temperature regime permits crops to grow throughout the year if moisture is available. The monsoon rains are usually copious, and in the dry season the main delta distributaries provide water for irrigation. The alluvial delta soils are highly productive, and deposition of silt from river water maintains their fertility. Relief is a very significant factor, for rice cultivation demands that a layer of water be retained on the land during the period of growth, and flat fields are essential for this.

Landholdings are very small – perhaps a hectare or less. Population density is very high. The level of technology is low – the soil, for instance, is turned by a simple wooden plough drawn by water buffalo. In the course of a year, two or perhaps three crops may be raised from the same plot of land. Rice shoots are transplanted individually by hand into the flooded paddy-fields. This is an indication of the immense labour input demanded by this type of farming. Land must be cultivated in this highly intensive manner if the small farmholding is to yield sufficient food to support the farmer and his family. For many there is seldom much surplus to sell. The typical farmer is very, very poor. He has little money to spend on improvements. At its simplest, this *intensive subsistence arable* farm economy may be represented by Fig. 70. It is a system that is particularly vulnerable to the natural hazards of flood and cyclone.

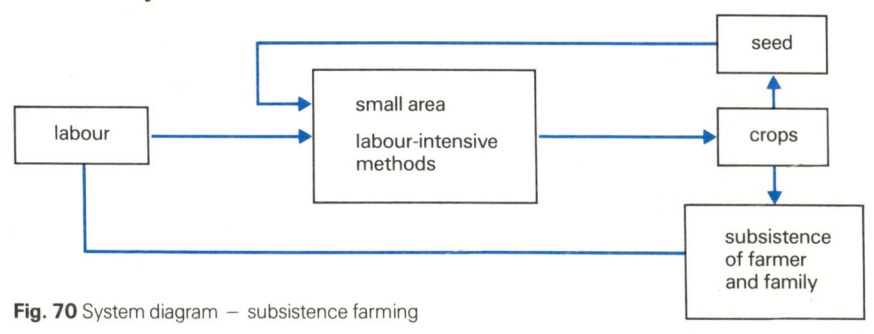

Fig. 70 System diagram – subsistence farming

Shifting Cultivation

This type of agriculture is a response by native peoples to tropical forest environments such as those of the Amazon Basin. Details may vary from region to region and tribe to tribe, but common characteristics are:

1. dense vegetation is attacked by fire – in the least wet season;
2. crops, such as manioc, are planted by hand in the ash-enriched soil of small, rough clearings.
3. the crops (and weeds) grow rapidly in the equatorial climate (Fig. 24, page 27) and are harvested when required, for storage is difficult, again because of climate;
4. after a short period, perhaps as short as two years, the clearing is abandoned, a new one created, and the cycle of shifting cultivation is repeated.

The cultivator must 'shift' because:
- clearance of the vegetation stops the addition to the soil of nutrients from the decay of forest litter;
- the ash and the soil's very limited natural stocks of nutrients are soon leached away by heavy tropical rains;

Plantation Agriculture

- the soil soon becomes so infertile that it will not yield worthwhile crops, and so the cultivator must move on – the clearing is reclaimed by the forest and after decades of recovery, may be cultivated again. Thus this type of *subsistence economy* depends upon the availability of a large amount of land. Cultivation is very *extensive*.

Today, this simple, primitive, arable enterprise is in great danger from the extension into the forests of 'modern' agriculture, which is less in tune with the constraints of this very delicately balanced natural environment. The rain forests are under threat.

Plantation Agriculture

This is an example of *large-scale commercial cultivation* found in tropical areas. Rubber (Malaysia) and tea (India, Sri Lanka) are commonly tested examples. These characteristic features of plantation agriculture should be noted:

- Plantations (or estates) are of large size. Commonly they are 1000 hectares or more.
- Land use is dominated by a single crop.
- The crop is mainly destined for export markets, hence plantations are sited close to transport facilities.
- Modern scientific production methods are used, e.g. plant breeding, pest control.
- Many operations are labour intensive (rubber tapping, tea picking). The large labour force is often housed in a village within the plantation.
- The crop undergoes simple processing on the plantation before despatch to market.
- Plantations often represent investment by multinational companies from 'advanced' Western countries of Europe and North America.

Agricultural Change

Changes in agriculture and their consequences are often the subject of examination questions.

In Britain:

- Increased use of machinery has led to the reduction of the labour force.
- To make full economic use of today's larger and more costly machines:
    i) small farms are combined into larger landholdings, leading to an increase in average farm size;
    ii) hedgerows have been 'grubbed up' to create large fields which may be worked more efficiently by large machinery;
    iii) there is specialisation in fewer crops.

- The use of chemicals – fertilisers, pesticides, herbicides – has increased.
- New, high-yielding varieties of traditional crops such as barley have been introduced.
- The average yield of all crops has greatly increased.
- Animal husbandry is more intensive – increase in factory farming.
- There has been a growth of co-operative and contract marketing.
- Within the EEC, effective farming has led to the creation of surpluses which are put into store, e.g. butter and wheat 'mountains'. The farmer responds to policy changes designed to reduce the surpluses. For example:
    i) oil-seed rape is encouraged at the expense of cereals;
    ii) quotas are imposed on milk production;
    iii) farmers are paid to take land out of cultivation.

Farming changes may have far-reaching consequences. People other than farmers may justifiably be concerned. We all have an interest in the countryside.

- Nitrates may increase crop yields, but they are a source of river pollution.
- Removal of hedgerows may liberate more land for crops and make for more efficient use of machines, but:
    i) it destroys important wildlife habitats;
    ii) in many eyes, it destroys the natural beauty of many rural landscapes;
    iii) it increases the risk of soil erosion;
    iv) field enlargement may lead to the loss of traditional footpaths.
- The drainage of wetlands may create more arable land, but it destroys the breeding grounds of important bird species.

(Changes affecting agriculture in tropical regions are included in Chapter 13.)

Clearly, the farmer has a major impact on the environment. Often, as with drainage and fertilisation, the impact may be beneficial. In other cases it is damaging, perhaps destructive. Nitrate pollution is one example. More important, and of world-wide significance, is soil erosion.

Consider a slope. Under natural conditions the loss by mass wasting is balanced by additions due to weathering processes. The soil retains its depth. The farmer may upset this balance, especially where slopes are steep and rainfall is heavy. Clearance of vegetation removes the binding effect of roots. On bare earth, before a crop has taken hold, less rain can infiltrate, so more runs over the surface, carrying away precious topsoil as it does so. The flow is channelled into rills that are swiftly eroded into deep gullies that gash and destroy the farmland. Vast areas of land have been lost by erosion in this way in the Appalachian region of the USA, for example.

Wise farmers guard against the danger by:
- planting steep slopes with grass for pasture;
- ploughing parallel to the contours (*contour ploughing*), not up and down the slope;
- growing different crops in alternate strips (*strip cropping*).

Flat land may suffer soil erosion by the wind. When farmland is bare and dry in spring, and winds are strong, the finest, most valuable soil particles may be blown away. This occurred with devastating effect in the 1930s in the 'Dust Bowl' of the prairies of the USA. Today it is a serious danger in the enlarged fields of the cereal-growing areas of eastern England.

Pastoral farmers are not immune from the dangers. If pastures are overstocked with animals (especially in periods of low rainfall), more grass is grazed than grows. Overgrazing leaves bare, trampled patches which, when soil is dry, are completely exposed to the wind.

Points to Note

1. "Explain . . .", "Account for . . .", "Suggest reasons for . . ." are common openings to questions on farming. Appropriate selection from the list of factors that influence the farmer's choice (page 55) will often form the basis of a good answer.

2. "Changes in farming" is another frequent visitor to examination papers. Make sure you have a list in mind and look for evidence of them on the maps or landscape sketches that may be presented as part of the question.

3. Specific examples are expected in illustration. Your own studies will supplement the selection given in this chapter. So consolidate your knowledge – draw system diagrams, adding as much detail as you can.

4. Be clear in your mind about the meaning of the terms introduced in the chapter, and use them in description of your examples of farm economies.

5. Questions frequently link farming with climatic graphs of a particular region. Look again at the chapter on climate. Be on the look-out for links between temperature/rainfall and crop requirements.

6. Farming is a subject that gives opportunities for the testing of 'values' (page 4). Can you come to a balanced judgement on such topics as factory farming, use of chemicals, removal of hedgerows, etc. Try stepping into the farmer's wellies and arguing the case for the adoption of mechanised scientific agriculture. Then don the anorak of, say, a keen member of the Ramblers' Association, and present your point of view.

7 Energy Resources

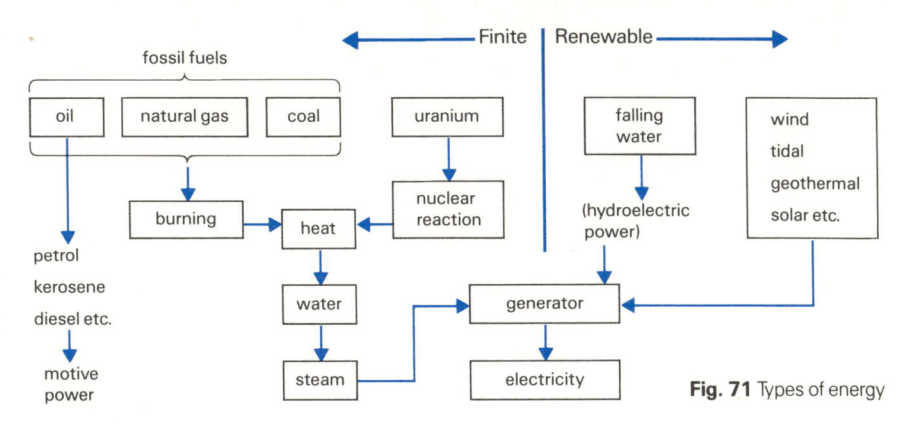

Fossil Fuels · Coal

Fig. 71 Types of energy

Energy, the power of doing work, has at present the variety of sources indicated in Fig. 71. Note the important distinction between *finite* and *renewable* resources. There is in the world only a fixed amount of finite resources (although there may, of course, be more yet to be discovered). As more energy is used, reserves decrease and costs and prices rise. We can foresee a distant time when resources will be totally used up. Renewable resources are those that are continuously available. Note the examples in the diagram.

Fossil Fuels

[handwritten note: coke — a solid-fuel product produced by distillation of coal to drive off the volatile constituents; used as a fuel]

Coal

Coal is the compressed, fossilised remains of rich vegetation that flourished in distant geological times. Fig. 72 illustrates features of its occurrence in the Ruhr coalfield of Western Germany.

Exploitation was encouraged by favourable circumstances:
- large extent of coalfield;
- high-quality coal – including much of good coking quality for the steel industry;
- thick seams;
- gentle dip;
- little disturbance of seams by faulting and folding.

These factors contributed to relatively low costs of extraction

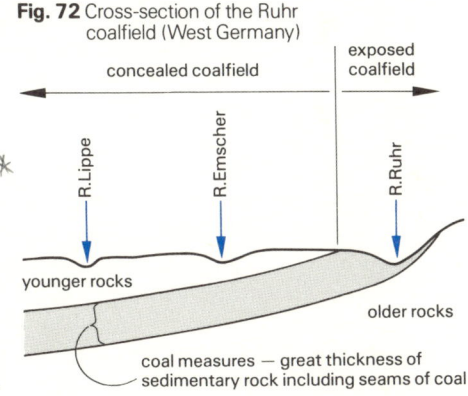

Fig. 72 Cross-section of the Ruhr coalfield (West Germany)

coal measures — great thickness of sedimentary rock including seams of coal

Mining

Naturally, mining started in the area of the exposed coalfield where seams outcropped at the surface. But every mine has a limited life – in time, its reserves become exhausted or too costly to extract. The mine must eventually close. The old, small mines of the Ruhr valley have long since closed and the industry has 'migrated' to the concealed coalfield where the coal is found at greater depth. Production is now concentrated in a small number of large, highly-mechanised mines.

Due mainly to strong competition from cheaper and more convenient oil and natural gas, demand for coal is in decline. So, too, is the number of mines, and the labour force. Thanks, however, to a high level of mechanisation in the remaining mines, output per man (*productivity*) is high.

Coal-mining makes a major impact on the environment. This is evidenced by:
- old, unsightly pit buildings and waste tips;
- surface subsidence and disturbed drainage;
- polluted rivers.

In the Ruhr, the planning authorities have devoted much effort to the improvement of the environment and have taken the various steps listed on page 80.

In many advanced countries, new development is increasingly influenced by environmental considerations. Objectors to the proposed opening-up of a new coalfield in the Vale of Belvoir, for instance, included:
- farmers – loss of agricultural land;
- residents – increased traffic, noise, dust;
- amenity/conservation groups – destruction of attractive landscapes, loss of wildlife habitats, etc.

A public enquiry had to weigh these objections against the claimed advantage of large quantities of low-cost coal, and the creation of employment, and general economic development.

An alternative to deep mining is *opencast mining*. Where seams are thick and close to the surface, overlying rock is removed and coal is extracted very cheaply by huge earth-moving machines. When the coal extraction operations have been completed, the overlying rocks and soil are replaced and the surface is landscaped or brought back into agricultural production.

The world distribution of coal is most uneven, for it is restricted to sedimentary basins of carboniferous age. It fuelled the growth of manufacturing in the advanced industrial countries of Europe and North America, where many fields are now exhausted or yield only costly coal. This has prompted an increase in trade. Thanks to cheap opencast mining, and efficient transport by special bulk carrier, coal can often be delivered from Australia to Europe often at less than the cost of domestic production.

Oil

Fig. 73 Anticlinal oil trap

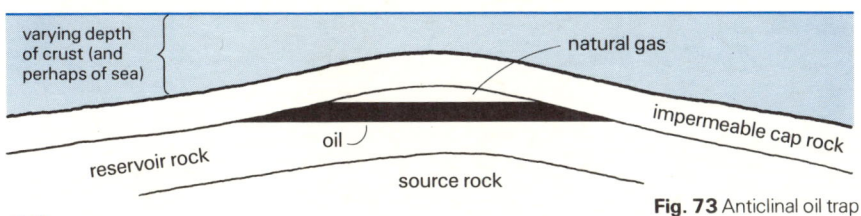

Oil

A typical occurrence is illustrated in Fig. 73. Microscopic marine organisms of ancient seas are thought to have died and decomposed into droplets of liquid and whisps of gas, which migrated upwards through porous rocks until stopped by an impermeable layer. Geological structures such as the anticline in Fig. 73 trapped gas and oil into accumulations, often of economic size.

Oil, like coal, and for similar reasons, has an uneven world distribution. Often, reserves are found in environments as hostile as frozen tundra, stormy seas or arid deserts. Demand is greatest in advanced industrial countries. Some, such as the UK, can meet most or all of their needs from domestic production. Others, such as Japan (*consumer nation*), must turn to those countries (*producer nations*) where production is much greater than domestic requirements. Oil is a large and vital item in world trade. Kuwait on the western shore of the Persian Gulf is an example of a producer nation. Favourable conditions allow low-cost production and marketing. In fields such as the Burgan field, rich accumulations can be easily and cheaply tapped by shallow wells. The copious yield is collected by pipes and delivered to a terminal on the nearby Persian Gulf for onward cheap transport by massive supertankers.

The oil from the well is 'crude' oil. Processed in a refinery, it gives a great variety of useful products. Important, of course, are fuels such as petrol, diesel and kerosene. In addition, crude oil yields a wide range of products, including fuel oil, waxes, lubricants and numerous chemical by-products which are raw materials for industries such as paint and plastic.

The refinery is vast in area and represents a huge capital investment. It must be carefully sited. The three main factors influencing the location of refineries using tanker-borne crude oil are:
1. large area of cheap, flat land;
2. sheltered waters deep enough to accommodate loaded supertankers;
3. proximity to markets for all diverse products, e.g. Fawley (Southampton Water) and Europort (Rhine).

Oil, like coal, has environmental impact. An oil refinery is not a pretty sight, and may well destroy the charm and amenity of lowland coastlines. Oil makes a worrying contribution to pollution of the seas.

Natural Gas

Natural gas has the uneven distribution of its fellow fossil fuels. One well-blessed area is sketched in Fig. 74.

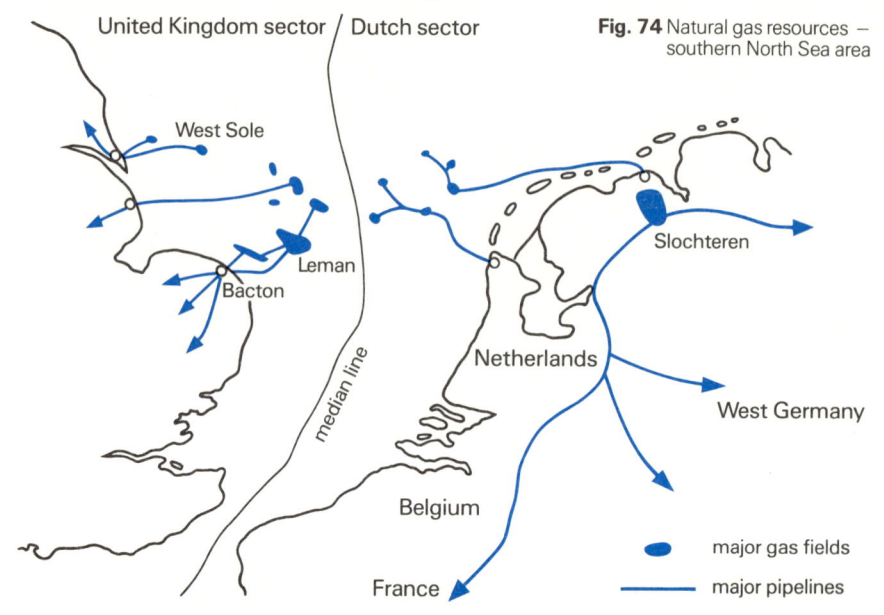

Fig. 74 Natural gas resources – southern North Sea area

Reserves at Slochteren were the first to be discovered and exploited, and now meet nearly half the energy needs of the Netherlands. Gas is exported by pipeline to France and Germany.

Deposits of gas trapped in strata beneath the sea are not so easy or cheap to exploit, for drilling rigs, production platforms and submarine pipelines are needed. They are all expensive items. In the southern North Sea, however, waters are relatively shallow and the distance from shore is not too great.

Natural gas needs no refining. After simple treatment at a terminal such as Bacton, it is fed into pipelines for direct distribution to home and factory. Environmental impact is minimal.

Electricity

At the heart of the power-station is the turbo-generator. As the shaft of the turbine rotates, so, too, does a powerful electromagnet set in a large coil of copper wire within the generator, and the current flows. Electricity is delivered by a grid of overhead powerlines to customers in home, office, factory, etc.

The essential rotation of the turbine may be achieved in a variety of ways.

Thermal Power-Stations

In a thermal power-station fossil fuels, especially coal and oil, are burned to produce the heat that turns water to steam, which, under pressure, is directed on to the blades of the turbine, so causing it to rotate. Large thermal power-stations, such as Fiddler's Ferry on the River Mersey near Warrington, can generate 2000 megawatts.

Factors influencing the location of thermal power-stations are:
1. large area of cheap, level land offering firm foundations for large structures;
2. large supplies of water for steam raising (pure) and cooling (river, sea);
3. availability of cheap and abundant supplies of fuel, e.g.:
   a) for coal – coalfield or coastal sites;
   b) for oil – close to refinery;
4. proximity to market (electricity is lost in transmission);
5. (coal only) – facilities for disposal of ash.

Nuclear Power-Stations

The nuclear power-station also uses turbo-generators, but differs in that a tightly-controlled nuclear reaction provides the heat needed to turn water to steam. Factors 1) and 2) above are important considerations in the location of nuclear power-stations, but as only small amounts of uranium are used, fuel transport costs are not a significant factor. Fear of accidents encouraged location of early stations away from populated areas, and coastal sites were sought as they could discharge low-activity liquid waste into the sea.

Hydroelectric Power-Stations

In hydroelectric power-stations, water falling under gravity is directed on to the turbine blades to cause rotation and the generation of electricity. It is the most familiar of the renewable sources of energy.

The potential of a site depends on the volume of water and the distance it falls (this is known as the *head of water*). The greatest potential for hydroelectric power (HEP) occurs at points where large rivers – e.g. Niagara – have a great fall. Potential is often less than ideal. Alpine rivers may have high heads of water, but volume is often small. Large lowland rivers seldom offer sites with high falls.

Heads of water may be created artificially with the construction of a dam and reservoir. A favoured site is a narrow section of a deep valley cut in tough impermeable rock. The reservoir evens out the flow of water and so smooths the production of electricity.

Potential for HEP, depending, as it does, so heavily on rainfall, rivers and relief, shows uneven world distribution. It is high at many points on the large rivers of equatorial areas in Africa, for instance. Up to now, only a fraction of the potential has been harnessed.

Environmental Factors

Uneven distribution is seen on a much smaller scale in Great Britain, where the Highlands of Scotland are particularly suitable. Favourable factors include:
- glaciated uplands:
  a) hanging valleys – naturally high heads of water;
  b) ribbon lakes for storage – often these lakes are enlarged by the construction of dams;
- high annual rainfall totals;
- lack of competition from alternative power sources.

HEP schemes often involve very heavy capital investment, but once established, no fuel costs are involved and so electricity can be generated relatively cheaply.

Multi-purpose schemes for river control – where the costs of dam construction are offset by benefits of flood control, irrigation and water supply as well as HEP – make for economic production of electricity.

Electricity and the Environment

The electricity industry has a major impact on the environment. Causes for current concern include:
- Tall pylons with their linking cables mar the beauty of rural landscapes.
- The large thermal power-station with its tall chimney and huge cooling towers is a visual blot on the landscape.
- The dam and reservoir needed for HEP production are also unsightly.
- The burning of fossil fuels liberates gaseous and solid pollutants into the atmosphere and makes a major contribution to acid rain.
- Nuclear power generation causes public debate on several points:
  i) build-up of radioactivity in seas;
  ii) problem of disposal of highly radioactive waste;
  iii) fears of accidents, such as that of Chernobyl.

Alternative Sources of Energy

Pilot - test (schemes)

The concerns connected with electricity generation, especially distrust of nuclear power, plus anticipation of future exhaustion of fossil fuels and their rising costs, have prompted a search for alternative and renewable sources of energy. Several have been identified, but development is small – often restricted to pilot schemes. It will be a long time before such sources can make a serious contribution to energy needs. This prompts many to the view that greater economy in the use of energy is essential, e.g. smaller cars, insulation of houses, etc.

Tides

On the Rance estuary in northern France, the rising tide passes through sluices in a barrage, to be trapped in a reservoir. When the tide falls, water is released to flow through turbines to generate electricity. The station can generate 62 megawatts of electricity – though not constantly.

The barrage carries a road across the estuary, but disadvantages include visual impact and interference with wildlife habitats.

Wind

Electricity is produced when the force of the wind rotates the blades of an aerogenerator. Wind as a force is free and everlasting, but:

- large numbers of tall supporting structures spoil landscapes (many of the windiest sites are in areas of natural beauty);
- areas of greatest average wind speed are in remote areas, e.g. north-west Scotland;
- electricity is not generated in periods of calm.

Waves

Techniques have been developed to convert ocean wave energy into electricity, but the scale would have to be enormous to meet a significant fraction of demand. Also, the supply of power, being dependent on waves, is irregular.

Sun

Electricity can be generated through solar cells and solar furnaces – but they are expensive and of limited value in cloudy areas.

Geothermal

In certain places, the Earth's crust is hot near the surface. Ground water is heated and, sometimes, turned to steam. This energy can be translated into electricity, but only locally, and with limited output.

Points to Note

1. Your attention is drawn to the locational factors given early in this chapter, for they are the basis of explanation. The course of the Trent is marked by a line of large, coal-fired, thermal power-stations. This is not a coincidence. Tick off the factors on your mental list – sites, water for cooling (river), cheap supplies of coal (nearby coalfields of south Nottinghamshire and Yorkshire), etc., and you have the basis of explanation.

Select examples of nuclear, oil-fired, and HEP stations, as well as oil refineries, and prepare explanations of location.

Points to Note

2. Power is at the heart of many environmental issues, so there is scope for the testing of values (page 4). The following topics are among those that prompt debate. Imagine yourself on each side of the fence in turn – for and against – and prepare your arguments.
    a) The opening of a new coalfield.
    b) A proposal to build a new power-station.
    c) A proposed barrage across the river Severn.
    d) Meeting the demand for electricity in the twenty-first century.
    e) The role of nuclear power.

Keep an eye on the media to update your information and provide new examples.

3. If coal figures prominently in your syllabus, prepare short studies of an expanding and a declining coalfield. Remember, as always, to locate your examples accurately.

8 Manufacturing Industry

Industry shows enormous contrast in scale. At one end of the range, a single worker labours at home or in a workshop with the simplest technology to turn out small quantities of a basic item (an enterprise known as a *cottage industry*). Then there are factories (or works, mills, plants) with complex, power-driven machinery employing anything from a handful to tens of thousands of workers. Some of the larger enterprises control a linked group of factories, and when these factories are in a number of different countries the term *multinational company* is used. The Ford Motor Company, for instance, from headquarters in Detroit, USA, controls car plants in more than 20 countries, with over 30 factories in the UK alone.

The Factory

The factory, like the farm, can best be understood as a system. Simple illustration is provided by Fig. 75, the components of which merit a word or two of explanation.

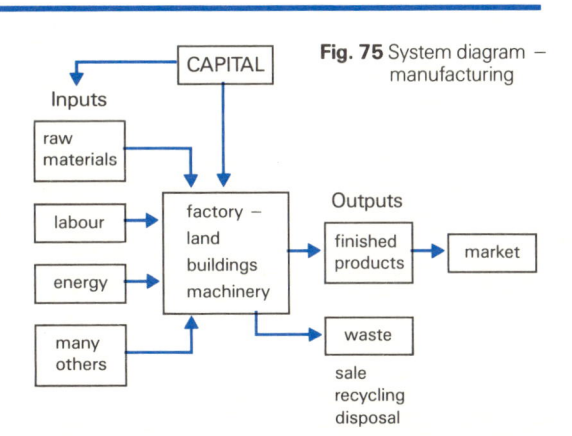

Fig. 75 System diagram – manufacturing

Capital
Capital is essential for building the factory, buying the machinery and financing the inputs. In advanced Western countries, capital is widely available (at the cost of *interest*). In Third World countries, lack of capital is a great handicap to industrial development.

Land
Land is important in that it controls the availability of suitable sites. The cost of land, too, is important, especially for major enterprises such as integrated iron and steel works which cover large areas.

Raw Materials
Raw materials may be as 'raw' as ore or wood, but increasingly they are processed or manufactured products. An *assembly* industry, such as car manufacture, uses the finished products of many industries (steel, glass, plastic, electrical, etc.) as raw material in the putting-together of its finished product.

Labour
Labour requirements are diverse. People with a wide variety of different skills are essential for the efficient operation of the modern factory.

Energy
Energy for most industrial enterprises is today supplied in the form of electricity and is available everywhere in advanced countries.

Outputs
The main factory output is, of course, the *finished product* or products. There may, however, be other outputs. For example, an engineering factory creates steel scrap which can be sold to the steel industry. A chemical factory, on the other hand, may produce waste that requires disposal. This may be difficult, and could be an added expense as chemical waste can be an environmental hazard.

Markets
The market – that is, the area in which the product can be sold – may vary in size. For some products it tends to be local, for others (increasingly) it is national or world-wide. The size of the market is important, because a larger market encourages greater output from the factory, which gives economy of scale, i.e. unit cost decreases as output rises. Sale in the market provides revenue, and subtraction of costs gives profit. Without profit, a factory cannot survive – unless it is subsidised in some way.

Transport
Transport is the basic linkage of all parts of the system from the assembly of the raw materials to the distribution of the finished product. Rail, road, and (within the factory) conveyor systems may all have a role to play. It is important to note that transport is often a crucial element in total cost, and hence in profitability.

Location of Industry
A factory must be sited with great care, for costs (and hence profits) can be greatly influenced by location. In establishing a new factory, the availability and/or cost of the following must be carefully considered:
1. land;
2. raw materials;
3. labour;
4. energy;
5. transport;
6. market.

Location of Industry

Government policy is an additional factor. Dominant in centrally-planned (communist) economies, it may also be significant in Western countries such as the UK.

It is the balanced evaluation of these factors that leads to a decision. In the aluminium smelting industry, for instance, the cost of energy is the prime consideration. Vast amounts of electricity are needed, and hence smelters seek locations close to cheap sources of power. For example, the large Kitimat smelter is served by the nearby HEP station at Kemano in coastal British Columbia, Canada.

Within the great variety of industry, we can recognise certain common types of location.

Raw-Material Oriented

These industries use large quantities of bulky raw materials which are expensive to transport, and hence sites where they may be assembled cheaply are favoured. A neat example is provided by the cement works near Hope in North Derbyshire (Fig. 76). Note how it snuggles between its two main raw materials. A third comes in by rail from the nearby Yorkshire coalfield. Proximity to markets, and availability of local labour, were other locational factors.

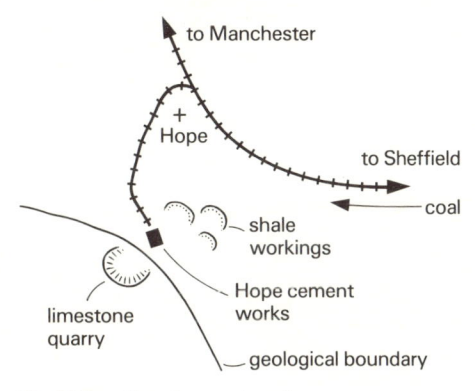

Fig. 76 Location of cement works

On a larger scale, the heavy chemical industry on lower Teesside is a good example. At extensive level sites served by good road, rail, pipeline and sea communications, large quantities are assembled of such varied raw materials as salt (local), limestone (Pennines), coal (Durham), potash (Cleveland), water (Tees and Pennines), natural gas (grid) and chemical feedstocks (oil refinery). Transport also assists in the distribution of highly varied output to markets in house and factory at home and overseas.

Market Oriented

Location close to major markets offers the advantages of:
- cheap and speedy transport of finished product to the consumer;
- close links between producer and consumer;
- availability of labour with diverse skills.

The market as a locational factor has grown in importance since the development of electricity made power available virtually everywhere, and since the car and lorry brought greater flexibility to transport. Market location is especially valuable when transport costs are higher on finished products than on raw material, e.g. brewing, soft drinks, baking, furniture. The rapidly expanding range of consumer goods, from washing-machines to cosmetics, from office machines to clothing, increasingly finds profitable locations close to major markets.

Footloose Industries

Some enterprises have a relatively free choice of location. They use raw materials in small quantities to manufacture products of great value in relation to weight. Transport costs are typically only a fraction of total costs and may therefore be largely ignored in choosing location. These can be called *footloose industries*.

Examples abound in the 'high tech' industries often based on microelectronics and biotechnology, and include computer hardware and software, robotics, weapons systems and telecommunications. These are often considered as the basis of a 'new industrial revolution'. They are described as *sunrise industries*, in contrast to the *smokestack industries* such as textiles and shipbuilding which depended on coal and rail in the nineteenth century.

One area where sunrise industries are of great importance in the UK is the so-called 'western corridor' – a wide strip flanking the M4 Motorway from London through Slough, Reading and Bristol to Newport in Gwent. Its attractions for footloose industry include:
- good communications – M4 Motorway, rail, and Heathrow Airport;
- close to several universities and research establishments;
- pleasing environment – landscape/climate;
- area attractive to essential, highly-skilled labour.

Industrial Estates

Modern industry, especially small or medium scale, footloose or market oriented, is increasingly located in industrial estates. These have the following characteristics:
- well designed, usually single-storey, factories;
- good layout – plenty of room for expansion;
- electric power and road transport – little pollution;
- wide variety of enterprises;
- commonly located on the edge of a built-up area which provides labour and, perhaps, the market.

Industrial Inertia

Note that an industry may persist in an area long after the factors that first encouraged location have ceased to be important. This is known as industrial inertia. The pottery industry first grew up in the Stoke-on-Trent area mainly because of the availability of cheap local clay and

suitable coal. Now the fuel is gas, and the clay (kaolin) comes mainly from Cornwall. The industry persists in the region because:
1. in the Stoke area there is a large reservoir of labour with the appropriate specialist skills;
2. the cost of relocation would be enormous, as factories etc. (fixed capital) would have to be abandoned.

Industrial Regions

Industry commonly clusters into relatively small areas clearly recognised as industrial regions. Common examples include South Lancashire, the Ruhr (West Germany) and the Damodar Valley (India). There are advantages in this clustering or, to be technical, *agglomeration*.
1. The finished product of one factory is often the input of another. If both factories are close together, transport costs are low, to the benefit of both. This is an oft-quoted example of *industrial linkage*.
2. The needs of a group of factories encourage the presence of other manufacturing or service industries. Engineering, for instance, may be attracted by the need for machines. Specialist services, such as transport, may also be established for mutual benefit.
3. The large population of an industrial region:
   a) provides a reservoir of labour with varied skills;
   b) provides a market for consumer goods, and so encourages new industry.

Note that the linkages that connect units in an industrial region to common advantage are not restricted to the transport of goods. Other examples include the movement of information by post, phone or facsimile machine and, of course, personal contact.

Industrial regions, having grown and developed, may stagnate and decline, and, in time, perhaps be rejuvenated. Factors contributing to industrial decline include:
- exhaustion of natural resources, e.g. coal, iron ore;
- reduction in demand for a product, e.g. railway locomotives;
- competition from foreign countries, e.g. cotton textiles (Lancashire), shipbuilding (Clyde and Tyne).

Long established and declining industrial regions show signs of age in their landscapes:
- obsolete 'smokestack' buildings on congested sites;
- network of narrow roads and streets ill-suited to modern road transport;
- unattractive environments marred by the scars of former activities, e.g. polluted rivers, decayed and derelict buildings, waste tips, old clay pits, quarries and surface subsidence.

Such characteristics contribute to a region's unfavourable image and sometimes discourage the establishment of new industry.

The decline of an industrial region has serious consequences. As factories close, unemployment rises, and personal incomes decline. There is less money to support local shops and services, which decline in their turn, with the loss of further jobs and income.

In the UK, declining industrial regions are found particularly in the North and West. Areas attractive to new and expanding industries are largely in London and the South-East. Significant contrasts may be identified. They can be measured in many economic indicators, such as:
- levels of unemployment;
- average incomes;
- car ownership;
- migration;
- house prices.

It must be stressed that these indicators represent average conditions and that differences may be small. But although small, these differences can be significant, and they prompt debate in the media on 'The North-South divide' and 'The two nations'.

Governments take steps, through their *regional policies,* to reduce these contrasts by:
- investment in infrastructure (e.g. motorways);
- establishment of new Government enterprises in the provinces, e.g. Royal Mint at Llantrisant in South Wales;
- building of factories in anticipation of need;
- financial incentives in the form of a variety of grants and allowances. These are available only in designated 'assisted areas'. In Great Britain, these incentives are greatest in the 'Development Areas' (e.g. Merseyside, Anglesey, parts of South Wales, etc.). Northern Ireland has separate and greater assistance, reflecting its more complex problems.

Regional policies have not eliminated regional contrasts, but have nevertheless enjoyed considerable success. New industries have been attracted to the regions, often from overseas. Examples include the production of television sets (South Wales) and motor cars (Washington, Co. Durham).

A new factory encourages further growth because it:
a) stimulates firms which manufacture component parts or provide essential services;
b) increases personal incomes, which stimulate local demand for consumer goods and services.

Thus the establishment of new industry can lead to an upward spiral of development.

The Ruhr

Fig. 77 The Ruhr industrial region

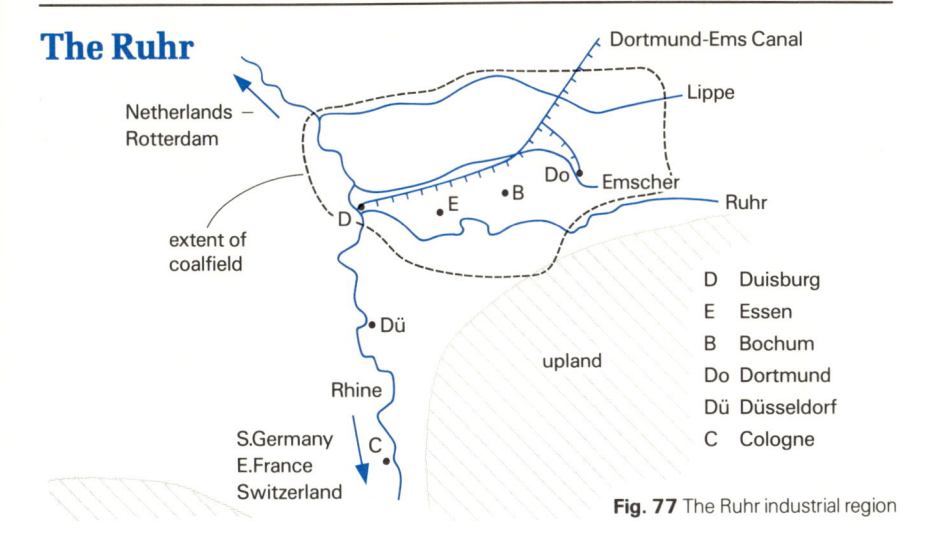

This major industrial region (Fig. 77) provides illustration of many of the above topics. After an early simple start on the southern edge of the coalfield, large-scale iron and steel manufacturing became established in the line of major towns between the Rhine and Dortmund, encouraged by:
1. good-quality coking coal at shallow depth;
2. cheap water transport (Rhine and wide canals) for import of rich iron ore and for the distribution of steel;
3. water for cooling;
4. an expanding market due to the development of steel-using industries, such as heavy engineering, armaments, etc.

The last factor is a particularly good example of the linkages that encourage the growth of an industrial region. Other examples include: coal as a raw material, as well as a source of energy for the chemical industry, part of the output of which is used by textile industries. Machinery manufacturing serves the full range of industry, and all benefit from the region's infrastructure of roads, railways and waterways.

The Ruhr in recent decades has seen many changes, including:
- Changes in the coal industry (page 66).
- Coal, steel, heavy engineering – indeed, all the traditional industries on which the Ruhr depended – have suffered contraction.
- The steel industry is now concentrated at sites along the Rhine where raw materials may be more easily and cheaply assembled.

Closure of mines and factories brought decline to the Ruhr. Incomes fell as unemployment rose. As in the UK, Governments attempted to stimulate redevelopment by the encouragement of new industry. This was hampered by the region's poor image caused by physical and visual

The Ruhr · Points to Note

pollution. The Ruhr Planning Authority works towards the repair of the damage and the improvement of the environment. Steps that are taken include:
- clearance of unsightly remains, e.g. pit-head gear, blast furnaces;
- landscaping of waste tips;
- green wedges (cf. green belts) keep built-up areas apart. Extensive tree planting improves amenity;
- creation of recreational facilities, e.g. water sports, in a number of Area Parks;
- establishment of purification plants on the heavily polluted rivers Ruhr and Emscher;
- urban improvements, e.g. new housing and shopping centres;
- strict control of air and water pollution.

These steps help to create the 'New Ruhr' image intended to attract new industry. Decline and unemployment are checked as modern industry, including car assembly, is established.

Points to Note

1. Some syllabuses specify particular industries for study. Check, and choose your examples accordingly. Be sure you can i) quote an example, ii) locate it accurately, iii) explain its location. For the last, have the list of factors (page 74) in mind.

2. Manufacturing industry is marked on OS maps (usually as *works*). So, too, are several important locational factors. Put the two together if asked for an explanation. Factors to look out for are land, transport, raw materials (e.g. quarry, clay pit), energy (mines, power-stations) and settlement (labour).

3. The same points can be made for photographs as for OS maps.

4. It is worth emphasising that industry, and industrial location, is subject to change. These changes reflect variations in economic conditions and advances in technology. Appreciate the contrasts. Have on hand examples of expanding and declining industries, and of regions of industrial growth and decline. For decline, the sad consequence of high unemployment should be especially noted.

5. The environmental impact of industry is worthy of attention. A factory creates wealth and provides employment, but may result in visual, noise or air pollution. Try to appreciate contrasting points of view and come to a balanced judgement. Consider, for instance, the proposed establishment of a new cement works on a rural site to windward of a large town where traditional industry is declining and unemployment is high.

6. The problems of industry in the Third World are considered in Chapter 13.

9 Recreation, Leisure and Tourism

In the UK and other advanced countries there has, in recent decades, been a great increase in leisure time, because of:
- a shorter working week;
- longer annual holidays;
- earlier retirement;
- more labour-saving machines in the home.

In the same period, higher incomes and greater mobility due to the increase in car ownership have given opportunity for wider and more varied use of this leisure/recreation time. It may include an hour or two in an urban sports centre, a day out at one of the growing number of 'Theme Parks' (e.g. Alton Towers) or stately homes (Woburn Abbey), or a week or more on holiday at destinations ranging from Blackpool to the Himalayas. Meeting the needs of the tourist is a large, varied and expanding service industry. It provides employment (though much is seasonal) and increases a country's earnings of foreign currency. It stimulates the growth of other activities such as farming, construction and the manufacture of gifts and souvenirs. Thanks to cheap air travel, the international tourist is travelling further afield. Many small and poor Third World countries offering sun, sand, sea and local colour look to the tourist industry as a stepping-stone to economic development (the Seychelles, for instance).

Traditional Resorts

Holiday resorts in the UK grew up in the nineteenth century. They expanded rapidly with the growth of cheap, quick rail transport and holidays with pay. Blackpool, for example, prospered because it had:
- sea, much sand, and fresh air;
- rail links to large industrial towns such as Bolton and Manchester;
- plenty of accommodation and entertainment, e.g. theatres, Blackpool Tower.

Land use in Blackpool is typically linear. The Promenade (extended seawards by piers) is flanked in turn by entertainments, hotels, boarding-houses, and residential areas.

The tourist industry, especially in the British climate, is seasonal. Blackpool has been more successful than most in extending its season. It does this by hosting out-of-season conferences, by providing attractions such as the autumn 'lights', and by offering cheap rates for accommodation at off-peak times.

Foreign Travel

New Destinations

Recent decades have seen great changes in the destination of the British holiday-maker. This is due to the development of air travel (especially charter flights) and the package holiday, by which accommodation and travel are organised together, usually at an attractive price.

The most popular destination is now the Mediterranean coastlands, especially the Spanish costas and islands. The low cost of package holidays is one reason. Others include:
- guaranteed dry, sunny summers;
- short travel time;
- sandy beaches and warm seas;
- cheap drink and night-life;
- attractive coastline and inland scenery;
- places of interest to visit.

The tourist industry is of great economic importance to Spain (nearly 50 million visitors a year), since it:
- earns large amounts of foreign currency;
- provides much direct employment, e.g. hotel staff, taxi drivers, etc.;
- stimulates other industries, e.g. construction, clothing, souvenirs;
- prompts expansion of infrastructure, e.g. roads, that may be shared by all;
- leads to a general increase in living standards.

But there are disadvantages.
a) Much of the employment is only seasonal – hence the offers of very cheap, out-of-season holidays in the mild winters.
b) The summer influx puts pressure on services, e.g. water, waste disposal, etc.
c) The holiday facilities (e.g. tower-block hotels) may visually harm the environment.
d) There is congestion and noise.
e) There is a breakdown of the traditional way of life.

The expansion of overseas holidays has had a marked effect on traditional UK resorts.

1. Many have suffered serious decline in prosperity as the number of visitors has fallen.

2. Visits tend to be shorter – second (short) holidays, weekend breaks, day trips.

3. There has been a growth in self-catering accommodation – flats, caravans, etc.

4. There is greater provision, in some resorts, of 'all-weather' entertainments.

Countryside

Leisure is increasingly spent in the countryside. The most attractive areas of our varied and beautiful country are conserved for the pleasure of this and future generations. Planning controls prevent harmful developments on *'heritage coasts'* (e.g. South Cornwall, Northumberland), in *'areas of outstanding natural beauty'* (e.g. the Cotswolds, the South Downs), and most particularly, of course, in the *National Parks*.

National Parks

These are defined by Act of Parliament as, "areas of great natural beauty giving opportunity for open-air recreation, established so that natural beauty can be preserved and enhanced, and so that enjoyment of the scenery by the public can be promoted". Note the twin objectives laid down by parliament:

1. conservation;
2. promotion of use.

There are eleven National Parks in England and Wales, but as yet none in Scotland. They contain varied but always beautiful landscapes:

1. Snowdonia, Lake District – glaciated uplands.
2. Dartmoor, Exmoor, Northumberland, Brecon Beacons, North York Moors – rolling moorlands.
3. Peak District, Yorkshire Dales – limestone scenery.
4. Pembrokeshire Coast – coastal scenery.
5. The Broads – freshwater wetlands.

The National Parks offer a wide variety of recreational activities, including walking, climbing, camping, cycling, caving, bird-watching, sailing, and fishing. They include places of interest to visit, such as charming villages, ancient monuments and stately homes.

Characteristics common to National Parks:

- many are located in upland and highland areas to the north and west;
- most are within easy reach of major conurbations (London excepted);
- the land is *not* owned by the Government – over 80% is in private hands;
- local populations depend on the areas for their livelihoods, e.g. farming, quarrying, forestry, tourism;
- the public does not have unlimited rights – access to all but open fell and moor is restricted to rights of way;
- planning powers ensure that proposed changes are not harmful to the landscape.

83

Conflicts in the National Parks

National Parks Authorities do not have an easy job. There are sources of conflict:

Conservation v. Use. Because of increased leisure, car ownership, and motorways, the number of visitors is increasing rapidly. This increased pressure on the Parks causes problems (attempted solution in brackets):
- footpath erosion (diversions, artificial surfaces);
- litter (serviced picnic areas);
- road congestion (car-parks).

The problems are greatest at the so-called 'honey-pots' – the places of greatest attraction, e.g. Malham Cove (Yorkshire Dales). Attempts to reduce congestion and ease the problems include:
- provision of car-parks, toilets and picnic areas (screened by trees to preserve the environment);
- road restriction and 'park and ride' schemes;
- promotion of alternative attractions.

Conservation v. Development. A proposed mine, quarry etc., favoured by the local population as a source of employment, may be considered harmful to the environment by conservationists.

Local Population v. Visitors. Local populations are affected by congestion, trespass, noise, vandalism, litter, (but for many the tourist industry is their livelihood).

Also, many cottages are purchased as second homes and holiday homes by town dwellers. This forces up property prices to the disadvantage of the local population, especially young couples setting up home.

Points to Note

1. Have another look at Chapter 3, especially page 26 onwards. Its content has a clear link with recreation and tourism and contributes to explanation. For instance, the climate of Mediterranean coastlands (Fig. 27, page 29) in both summer and winter is a great attraction for the holiday-maker. It is Blackpool's handicap (and that of other UK resorts) that it lies in the latitudes of prevailing westerly winds which bear depressions and bring the most variable weather.

2. There are similar profitable links to be made with landscape. The attractions of coastal scenery are the result of rock and process. To many people, the scenery of limestone accounts, in part, for the attraction of the Yorkshire Dales National Park.

3. The advantages and disadvantages of the growth of the tourist industry in Spain (page 82) may equally well be applied to other countries, such as Greece and Turkey.

4. OS maps lend themselves to the testing of the topics in this chapter. They present a picture (in symbols) of the features of country and coast that are attractive to tourists and holiday-makers. Included, too, shaded in blue, are features such as viewpoints, beauty spots, stately homes, etc., that the tourist may wish to visit.

5. Don't hesitate to quote examples, from your own experiences, of recreation and tourism.

6. Topics in this chapter may give rise to much public debate. Be sure you can fairly present both sides of the conflicts that occur within National Parks.

10 Transport

Transport is the movement of people and goods over distance. It can be measured not only in kilometres but also, and usually more significantly, in cost and time. On a trip into town, for instance, you are more concerned about fare and length of journey than about the number of kilometres covered.

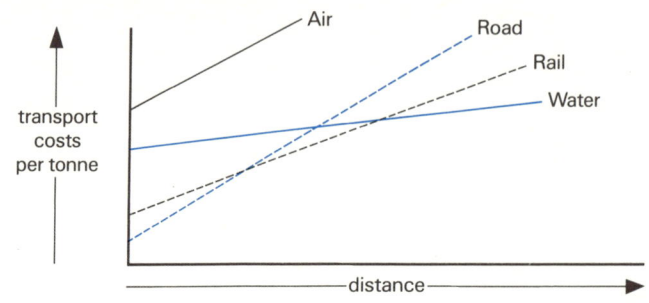

Fig. 78 Transport costs vary with mode and distance

Time taken reflects the speed of transport, which varies with the mode: this can range from a sluggish barge to a supersonic aircraft. Cost of transport varies with mode and distance (Fig. 78). The different points of origin on the vertical axis represent the different *fixed* costs, i.e. the costs of providing equipment and terminal facilities. These, added to *running* costs (largely wages and fuel), which vary with distance, give *total* costs. It will be appreciated that road transport is cheaper than rail transport over short distances.

Routes

The route followed by a line of communication is influenced by the need to:
1. maximise traffic – hence routes are attracted to urban and industrial regions;
2. minimise construction and operating costs.

The nature of the land surface is important. Gentle gradients are sought by road and, especially, rail – hence valleys and gaps are favoured, but steep slopes and marshes are avoided. If traffic warrants, obstacles may be overcome by bridge, tunnel, cutting, or embankment.

The availability of transport facilities varies greatly from area to area. Many less developed countries are dependent largely on animal traction or human porterage. Advanced countries such as the UK are, for most of their areas, closely served by the full range of transport modes – road, rail, water, air and pipeline.

Roads

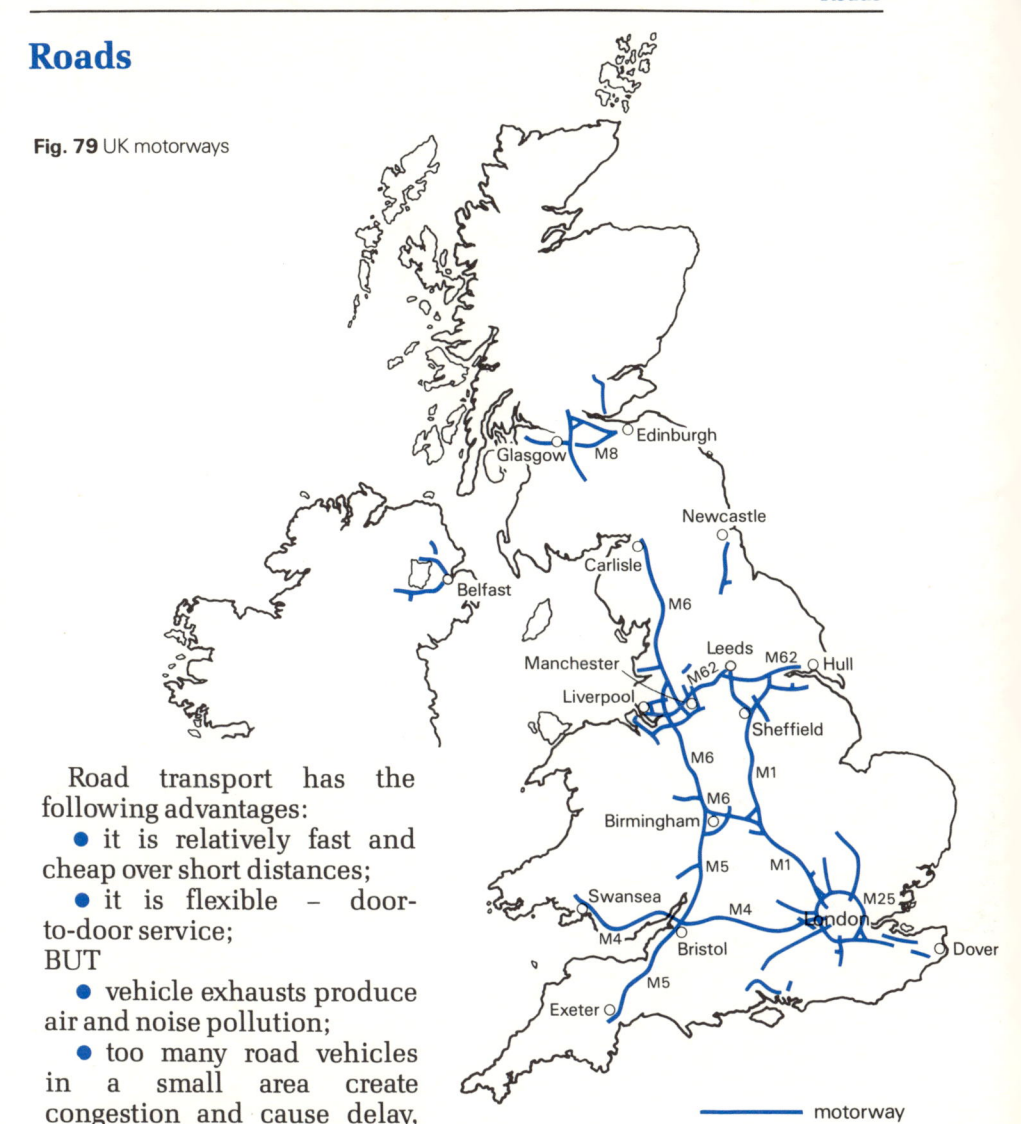

Fig. 79 UK motorways

Road transport has the following advantages:
- it is relatively fast and cheap over short distances;
- it is flexible – door-to-door service;

BUT
- vehicle exhausts produce air and noise pollution;
- too many road vehicles in a small area create congestion and cause delay, e.g. town centres;
- small load size limits usefulness.

This last point has been alleviated by the large 'juggernaut' lorry which can carry 38 tonnes, and which has extended the range of economic road transport. Such vehicles, however, are not without environmental problems on traditional roads, especially where these are narrow or pass through towns. Such large lorries are, of course, better suited to motorways – roads specifically designed for the most efficient and speedy use of road vehicles.

Networks

Fig. 79 shows the motorways in the UK. The following points about the pattern should be noted.
 1. They link major areas of population and industry.
 2. They also provide links to holiday areas (Devon, the Lake District) and ferry ports (Dover).
 3. There is a marked focus on London.
 4. London and the West Midlands have ring motorways.
 5. They follow lowland routes (but the M62 is an exception).

Motorways are appreciated for the safe and swift transport they encourage, but they are not without environmental implication. Proposals for new motorways may bring objections from a variety of groups, including:
- farmers – loss of land, splitting of farms;
- amenity groups – damage to attractive rural landscapes, loss of wildlife habitats, loss of footpaths;
- householders near a proposed route (especially in urban areas) – noise, air pollution, etc.

Networks

Look again at Fig. 79. It will serve as an example of a transport *network*. Places and junctions are known as *nodes* and the lengths of motorway between them are *links*. Divide the number of links by the number of nodes and you have calculated the *beta index*. The higher the value of the index, the greater the network's *connectivity* – one measure of its efficiency. The beta index enables us to compare networks and note changes with time.

A node which is well served by links is said to be *accessible*. From D in Fig. 80, every other node can be reached by travel on a total of 11 links. No other node in the diagram has a figure so low. Node D, then, has the greatest accessibility. The figure 11 is D's *Shimbel index*, a measure of the accessibility of the network as a whole.

Divide the total length of a network by the area it covers and you have a figure for *network density*. High densities are a feature of advanced countries, such as those of Europe. Low values of network density, and the economic handicaps it implies, reflect the simple skeletal transport system of much of the Third World.

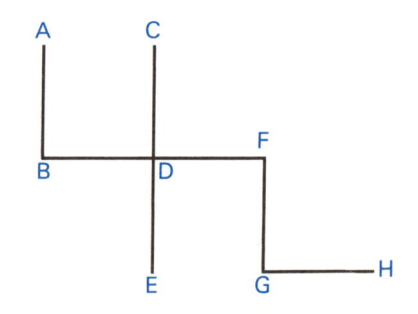

Fig. 80 Diagrammatic transport network

Roads and Development in the Amazon Basin

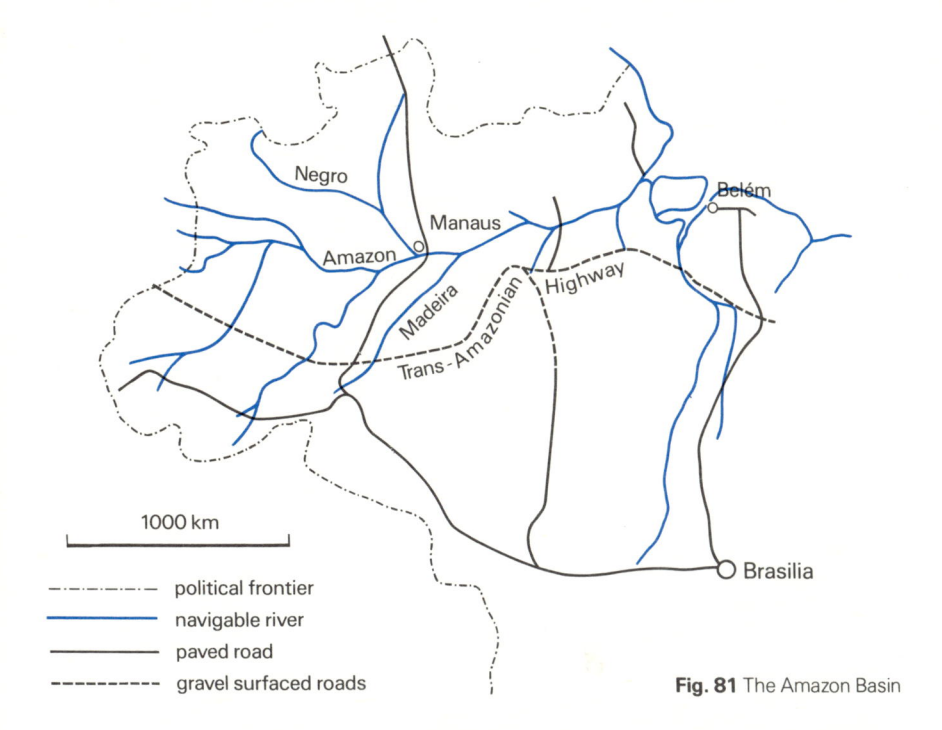

Fig. 81 The Amazon Basin

Roads were chosen by the Brazilian Government to supplement navigable waterways in efforts to open up the forests and savannas of the the Amazon Basin (Fig. 81). Relatively low costs of construction influenced this choice. Trees could be cheaply cleared by mechanical means and, initially, gravel surfaces would suffice. The aims of the development are to:

1. provide access for HEP and mining enterprises;
2. encourage agriculture on small farms, so attracting landless peasants from overpopulated parts of Brazil, especially the dry North-East;
3. encourage agriculture on large-scale enterprises, such as plantations and cattle ranches, so providing export crops;
4. integrate the remote areas more closely with the rest of Brazil.

One result of these developments is enormous deforestation, which is causing great concern. Road construction, cutting a wide swathe through the forest, leads to the loss of trees. So, too, do mining, HEP reservoirs, and housing. The 22 smelters which treat iron ore from the Carajus mine have a vast appetite for charcoal which is made from the virgin selva (rain forest).

The greatest destruction, however, stems from the extensive burning of the forest to produce farmland and pastures. The consequences include:
- loss of the soil's already limited natural fertility by leaching and by a reduced level of organic input;
- serious soil erosion on sloping land;
- loss of livelihood and, perhaps, life, by native Indian shifting cultivators (page 61);
- fears that plant and animal species may become extinct as a result of widespread forest destruction;
- suspected damage to the atmosphere by increased levels of carbon dioxide (the 'greenhouse effect', leading to an increase in world average temperatures).

Railways

Advantages
- Fast service between fixed points.
- Comfortable passenger transport.
- Suited to the cheap movement of large quantities of bulky goods, e.g. coal, ore.
- Create little pollution.

Disadvantages
- Expensive to construct and maintain.
- Inflexible.

The railway was the dominant form of land transport in the nineteenth and early twentieth centuries. Competition from road transport has brought decline. Today, rail transport specialises in the following tasks for which it is best suited:

1. high-speed movement of passengers between large towns (inter-city);
2. long-distance and regular transport of goods, (e.g. non-stop 'merry-go-round' trains which take coal from mines to power-stations);
3. commuter services into large urban centres, e.g. London;
4. movement within large urban areas – mainly underground (e.g. London tube or Paris Métro).

Sea Transport

Advantages
- Very cheap – especially over long distances.
- Large load capacity – especially with modern bulk carriers.

Disadvantages
- Very slow.
- The apparent flexibility of the open sea is restricted by the need for terminal port facilities. As the average size of ships increases, these facilities become fewer.

The southern North Sea (Fig. 82) illustrates a variety of port types.

Grimsby – fishing port.
Dover – ferry port.
London – traditional port that has suffered great decline because of the increase in the average size of ships and new transport methods.
Felixstowe – expanding as it takes advantage of:
  1. containerisation (page 93);
  2. ro-ro (roll-on roll-off – ship accommodates loaded lorries);
  3. short sea crossing to major markets of Europe;
  4. easy access to Rotterdam/Europort – world's busiest port (see page 92). It is an *entrepôt* because it serves areas beyond national frontiers.

Fig. 82 Ports of the southern North Sea

Inland Waterways

The qualities of sea transport are shared by inland waterways (rivers and canals) but on a reduced scale. The Rhine (Fig. 83) is one of the world's busiest inland waterway systems. There are several reasons for this.

1. The length of the Rhine waterway is exceptional. The *head of navigation* (the furthest inland point a vessel may reach) for barges is Basle in Switzerland. The head of navigation for ocean-going vessels is Cologne.

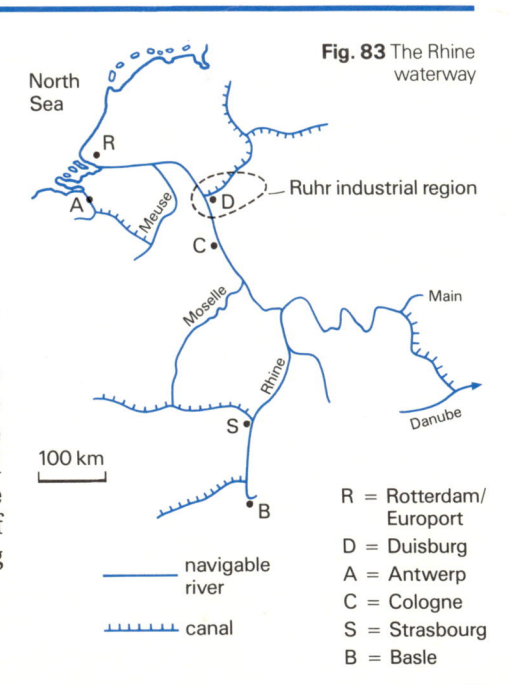

Fig. 83 The Rhine waterway

R = Rotterdam/Europort
D = Duisburg
A = Antwerp
C = Cologne
S = Strasbourg
B = Basle

2. The importance of the Rhine is extended by a number of navigable tributaries and large canals.

3. The area served by the waterway is densely populated and highly industrialised, so that much traffic is generated. Commodities which benefit greatly from the low transport costs include coal, ores, petroleum products, building materials.

4. It is well served by the major seaport of Rotterdam/Europort with its international connections.

Navigation on the Rhine does, however, face certain problems.
- There is seasonal variation in depth.
- Narrow gorge sections can lead to congestion.
- Upstream movement is hampered by strong currents.
- Ice is occasionally a problem in extreme winters.

Contrast is afforded by the Amazon Basin (Fig. 81). This major river, with its huge tributaries, drains the heart of the continent of South America. Ocean-going ships can reach Manaus almost 1500 km from the open sea. But the region is only thinly peopled and little developed, so traffic is light.

Rotterdam/Europort

This port's position between sea and inland waterways is evident from Fig. 83. The reasons that contribute to its position as the world's number one port include:

1. The area it serves (its *hinterland*) is:
    a) very large;
    b) well served by road, rail, waterway and pipeline;
    c) densely populated and heavily industrialised – much traffic is generated.

2. The port offers safe accommodation for the largest ships. It has expanded westwards from its original site at Rotterdam to the extensive deepwater development of Europort which meets the needs of the largest ships.

3. The port has been quick to adapt to technological development and provides the special facilities needed by container, ro-ro, and bulk carriers.

4. The port has earned a reputation for speed and efficiency.

5. Rotterdam/Europort is a *break of bulk point*, i.e. a point where large inward cargoes are split into smaller loads for onward despatch by other modes of transport. Break of bulk points are favoured sites for industries based on imported raw materials. Rotterdam/Europort is no exception, and oil refining and food processing are important industries of this type. Other industries which contribute to the importance of the port include petrochemicals and ship repair.

Air Transport

Advantages
- Very high speed – especially suited to long-range passenger transport.
- Can provide transport in remote regions, e.g. Northern Canada, Australian outback.

Disadvantages
- Expensive.
- Journey times from airport to city centre are often considerable.
- Economic cargoes are limited to high-value light items, e.g. precious metals, precision machinery, electronic equipment, etc.

The factors influencing the location of airports (e.g. Heathrow) include:
1. a large area of level land, preferably not prone to fog;
2. proximity to an urban centre (e.g. London);
3. good transport links (motorways, London Transport);
4. environmental considerations, such as noise and the loss of a large area of land.

Containerisation

This integrates the use of various transport modes. Goods are securely packed in locked metal boxes of standard sizes which can be cheaply carried by, and transferred between, various transport modes, thus gaining the advantages of them all – speed, safety and reduced costs.

Points to Note

1. In some syllabuses, transport enjoys a section all to itself – and hence has its own questions in the examination papers. Otherwise, transport is tested in relation to other topics. Common examples include location of industry, siting and growth of settlements, traffic problems in cities, access to National Parks, etc.

2. The modes of transport are in constant competition. Cost and time are important, and for passenger traffic, comfort and convenience are other considerations. Be aware of the advantages and disadvantages of each mode. Don't hesitate to draw on your own experiences.

In this competition the unsuccessful suffer. Rail, for instance, has suffered greatly at the hands of road transport. Today's rail network is only a shadow of its former glory.

New developments influence the transport balance. Consider the likely effects of the opening of the Channel rail tunnel on ferries and ferry ports, air and road traffic.

3. Be ready with definitions of transport terms such as entrepôt, hinterland, head of navigation, bulk carrier, container, etc.

4. Other transport networks can, of course, be measured in the same way as roads (page 88). Major contrasts occur between countries – especially between developed (Western) and developing (Third World). Contrasts are also evident within countries – e.g. between the Highlands of Scotland and the Midlands of England. Can you explain this contrast?

5. Prepare an evaluation of the environmental impact of the various modes of transport, e.g. visual, air, and noise pollution. A topical aspect is the drive to introduce unleaded petrol.

6. Transport may be linked with OS maps. Topics worthy of thought include:
   i) the influence of relief and drainage on the course of road, rail, etc.
      – e.g. points selected for bridges, avoidance of marshes, etc.;
   ii) location and times of possible road congestion, e.g. small country towns on market days.

1 Settlement

Settlements come in a wide range of sizes:
Isolated Residence – a farm, for instance.
Hamlet – a small cluster of buildings – not containing any services.
Village – a larger cluster, one that includes at least one service, such as church, shop, inn.
Town — a still larger cluster with a range of shops and services.
Conurbation – a very large built-up area caused by the growth and merging of a number of separate towns.

Note that these terms do not lend themselves to precise definition. For example, there is no clear-cut dividing line between village and town. The population of the latter may range from, say, three or four thousand to many hundreds of thousands. 'City', too, is imprecise. It is used, for instance, to describe the financial area of London. Often the word is used as a shorthand term meaning a large urban area.

Rural Settlement

Rural settlement is concerned with the three smaller units in the list, the farm, hamlet and village (though sometimes a small market town may be considered).

It is important to distinguish between:
Site – the land on which a settlement is built;
Situation – the broader landscape in which the site is set – its relationship with the surrounding area.

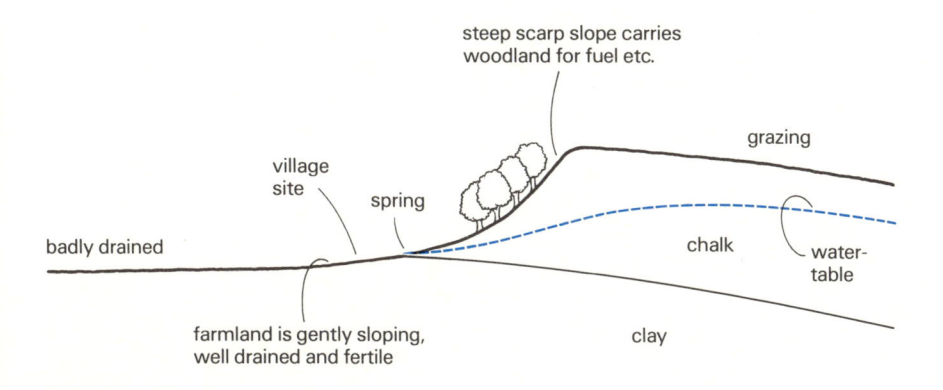

Fig. 84 Sketch section illustrating settlement site

Villages

Most village sites in the English lowlands were chosen before the Norman invasion of 1066. They were chosen by farming folk with the requirements of their subsistence form of agriculture in mind. Factors of influence were:
- availability of land – arable and pasture (fertile soil obviously being favoured);
- water supply – river, well, or spring;
- freedom from the risk of flooding, i.e. dry point;
- woodlands for building material and fuel;
- shelter;
- security (in troubled times and areas).

Favoured sites included well-drained terraces along major rivers, and the lower scarp slopes of cuestas – as in Fig. 84.

Common words used to describe village shape or *morphology* are:
- *compact* – buildings clustered closely together;
- *linear* – arrangement of buildings in line, usually either side of a road;
- *loose knit* – buildings scattered within the parish area.

It is important to distinguish between *settlement* (e.g. a farm, hamlet, village, etc.) and *settlement pattern* (the nature and arrangement of settlement over an area). Two common types of settlement pattern are:
- *dispersed* – where the population of an area mainly live in isolated houses or small hamlets;
- *nucleated* – where the bulk of the population live in villages.

Settlement and settlement patterns are *dynamic* – they alter with time and changed circumstances. Deep in Britain's rural areas, for instance, employment opportunities have declined and continue to decline with the increased mechanisation of agriculture. Many village dwellers, especially the young, move to the towns in search of work. Village population may fall below the level needed to support school, shop, Post Office and bus route. These closures, in their turn, encourage further loss of population. It is a downward spiral of decline.

In some areas, efforts are made to stem the flow by encouraging such activities as forestry, rural crafts, tourism, etc. In contrast, villages near a town may experience an increase of population with the 'in-migration' of commuters. Old cottages are refurbished and extended, new high-cost housing is built. This causes house prices to rise above the level that the local population can afford.

In attractive and popular rural areas – the highlands of mid and north Wales, for example – houses are sought by retired urban folk and by others for weekend and holiday accommodation. Here again, increased demand causes a steep rise in house prices, which leads to ill-feeling (even conflict) on the part of some elements of the local population.

The Growth of Towns

Towns develop, usually from a village nucleus, for a variety of reasons – perhaps the most important being their role as centres for the provision of services for their inhabitants and the population of the surrounding area. Services are provided in advanced societies in bewildering variety. Retailing, wholesaling, administration, education, law and entertainment are a few broad groupings. You avail yourself of a service when you buy a loaf, have a haircut, go to school, visit the cinema, post a letter, attend a concert, travel by bus.

There are two important points to note about services – each has:

1. *range* – the distance people are prepared to travel to obtain the service;
2. *threshold* – the number of customers or clients needed to make the provision of the service profitable.

There is a gradation in services. At one end of the scale there are *low-order services*. They have small range and low threshold. People are not prepared to travel far for a low-order service; its market area is small; it serves only a local area. Newsagent, butcher and hairdresser are examples. In contrast, *high-order services* have large range and high threshold. Many people are prepared to travel a considerable distance for the service. The department store and theatre are examples.

Provision of services generates employment and stimulates the growth of settlements, but to different sizes. In an area, a *hierarchy* of settlements may be identified (Fig. 85). There are usually many small towns offering a few low-order services, hence having a small sphere of influence, with progressively fewer places offering a wider range of services. At the peak of the pyramid is a country's largest settlement, which if of truly dominant size, e.g. London, or Paris, is described as the *primate* city.

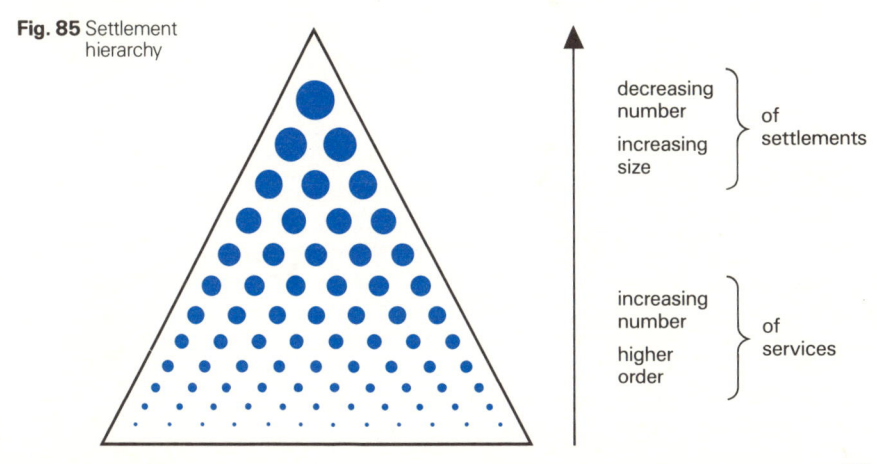

Fig. 85 Settlement hierarchy

Location of Towns

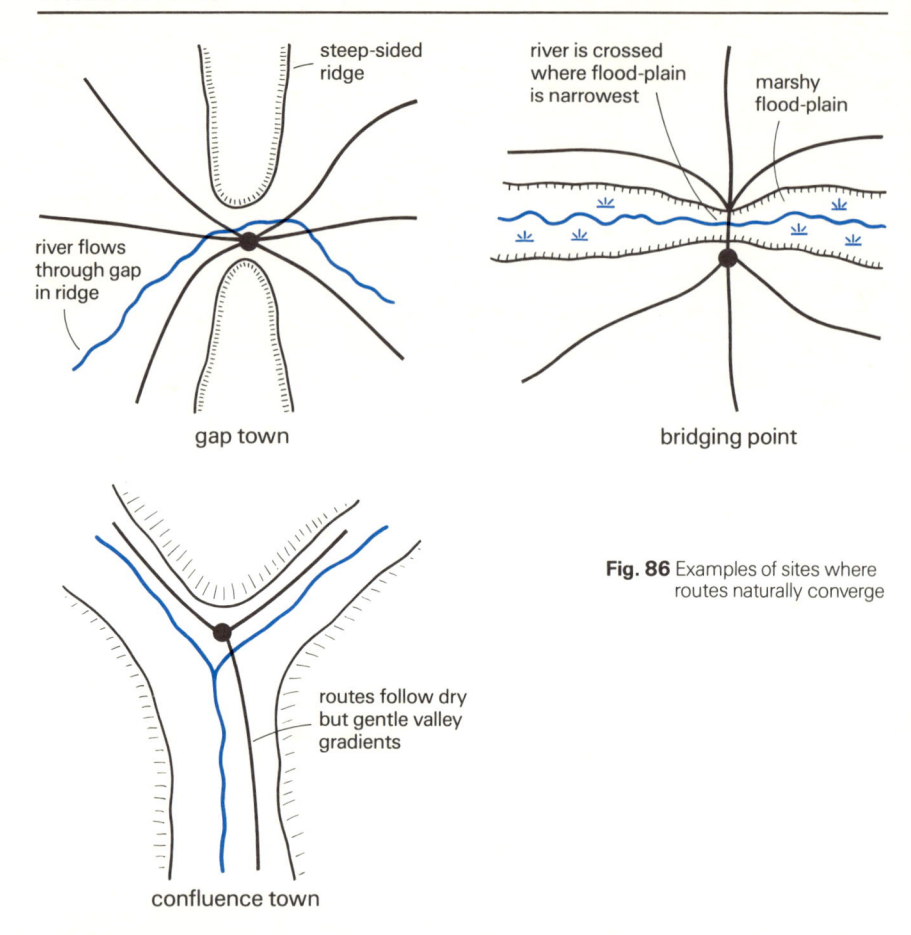

Fig. 86 Examples of sites where routes naturally converge

Accessibility is a key factor in the provision of services. All providers of services obviously want to be easily reached by as many potential customers as possible. They seek to locate where lines of movement meet. This is true for the corner shop. It is also the case in the growth of towns. Sites where routes naturally converge have high accessibility and hence are favoured for growth. Examples are given in Fig. 86.

The growth of a town may be encouraged by the development of functions other than the provision of services. Important examples are mining and manufacturing. Most towns have a range of functions; and, usually, the larger the town, the greater the range and importance of its activities. Capital cities are illustrations of this. In some cases, however, the dominant importance of one particular function gives a town a distinctive character. Examples are: St. Helens (industry), Blackpool (holiday resort), Felixstowe (port), Cambridge (education).

Patterns within Large Urban Areas

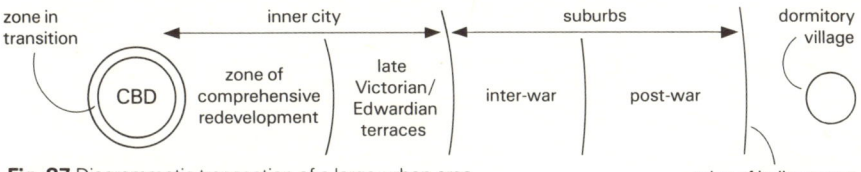

Fig. 87 Diagrammatic transection of a large urban area

Fig. 87 is a diagrammatic transect outwards from the centre of the typical large UK urban area. It locates distinctive patterns.

Central Business District (CBD)

This small but vital area lies at the heart of the urban area. Characteristic features of the Central Business District are:
- it usually includes the original settlement site;
- it is the focus of routes, natural and man-made, hence it is the most accessible part of the town;
- its high accessibility attracts a range of important functions – retail, wholesale, commercial, entertainment, etc., each largely concentrated in its own functional zone within the CBD;
- competition for central sites leads to very high land values, hence little open space and high buildings, e.g. tower office blocks;
- it is a major source of employment, yet has few residents, so has a twice daily 'rush-hour'.
- it is fringed by a zone of old and obsolete buildings known as the *zone in transition*.

It will be appreciated from Fig. 87 that by far the greatest share of the urban area is devoted to the residential function – but in zones of differing character.

Zones of Comprehensive Redevelopment

In the immediate post-war years, large areas of cramped, poor-quality, terraced housing were swept away. The population was rehoused in:

1. large local authority (council) estates (overspill) on the edge of the built-up area;
2. cleared inner-city land – here, the accommodation constructed was council flats, with all amenities in high-rise blocks, or in huge system-built constructions, often linked by high-level walkways. Blocks were well spaced but the population density was still high.

High-rise development did not prove as successful as anticipated because of:
- break-up of communities;
- isolation, especially of mothers with young children;
- constructional weaknesses, e.g. dampness, lift failures.

Later redevelopment has been in the form of low-rise estates.

Late Victorian and Edwardian Housing

In recent years there has been a trend towards retaining the typically long terraces built around the turn of the century on narrow rectilinear street grids of high density. Front doors open on to the street or perhaps tiny front gardens. Such houses have a yard rather than a garden at the back. Terraces of houses may be interspersed with a Victorian park, or with industry along the lines of communication. Such housing is now commonly improved by refurbishment: new roofs, windows, the installation of central heating, bathrooms and indoor lavatories. Refurbishment is less costly than comprehensive redevelopment of an area. No rehousing is necessary, so communities are not broken up. Such areas usually have the advantage of relatively low-cost housing and proximity to the CBD.

Inter-War Housing

Expansion of urban areas was made possible by the development in urban transport. Long terraces and straight streets were abandoned. The common unit became the semi-detached house, but rows of four were a feature of many council estates of the period. There were gardens back and front. Street plans were curved rather than straight; indeed, in many local authority estates the plan was precisely geometrical. Small culs-de-sac were a feature. Streets often had grass verges and were tree-lined.

Post-War Housing

The post-war era brought expansion of the built-up area, which was possible with improved bus services and especially the growth of private car ownership. Extensive local authority estates (overspill and others) of mixed housing were built; small units dominated, but maisonettes and blocks of flats were interspersed with these. Geometrical plans were abandoned, to be replaced by roads with gentle curves to give changing vistas. The element of grass verge and trees was retained. Private development continues to favour the semi-detached house, but detached houses in large grounds are a feature of high-cost development. Greater accommodation is now allowed for the motor car.

Suburban housing generally is more spacious, and the environment is considered to be more appealing than that of the inner city, but housing costs are higher and the time and expense of journeys to the centre of the town are a disadvantage.

Dormitory Villages

A dormitory village is an attractive village beyond the edge of the built-up area, expanded by the high-cost housing of commuters who can afford the long, daily journey to work.

Service and Shopping Centres

Urban Service Centres

In the large town, the variety of service centres indicated on the model (Fig. 88) may be identified.

○ CBD
● large suburban service centre
□ out-of-town shopping centre
• small suburban service centre

Fig. 88 Model of location of service centres in a large urban area

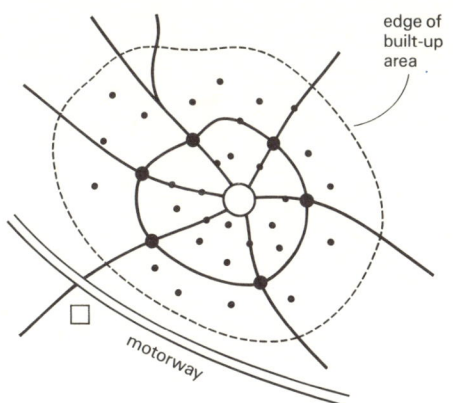

Small Suburban Service Centre

A small suburban service centre is a handful of establishments in a residential area, offering low-order (convenience) goods and services meeting frequent need. Typically, the shops include a small food shop, newsagent, sub post office, hairdresser, etc.

Large Suburban Service Centres

These are often located on the sites of old villages where radial and ring routes intersect. They offer the low-order services found in small service centres, plus a wide range of higher order, e.g. clothing, electrical goods, DIY, banks, building societies, estate agents, etc., with perhaps one or two supermarkets and chain stores.

The Central Business District

The CBD will have a large number and range of shops of high threshold. Department and variety stores are found near the point of maximum accessibility. Clothing, shoe, and jewellery shops are nearby, clustered together to benefit from comparison shopping. Specialist shops (e.g. books, art, outdoor activity) are on the edge of the shopping area. Convenience shops are rare.

In the CBD, services occupy a separate but adjacent zone of their own. High-order services such as banking, insurance and the legal profession, together with the area headquarters of numerous commercial and industrial undertakings, have their own share of the CBD, dominated by offices.

Out-of-Town Shopping Centres

These are a recent and continuing development, consequent upon the increase in car ownership. They comprise large, single-storey units with extensive car-parks, developed on sites offering cheap land and good road access. Typically, they are furniture, carpet and DIY stores, and hypermarkets.

Manufacturing

This is an important function of many large urban areas. Typical locations in the UK are indicated in the model (Fig. 89).

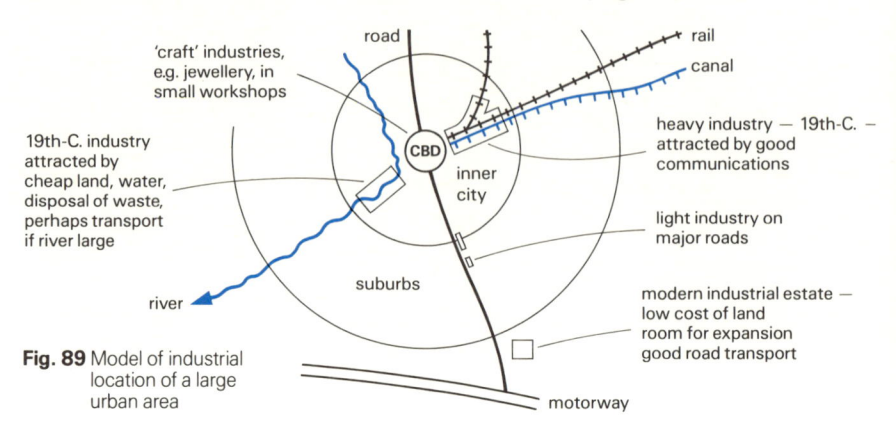

Fig. 89 Model of industrial location of a large urban area

Movements of Population

Fig. 90 is a model of population movements common to large UK urban areas. The broken lines (1) represent a vast number of daily journeys to and from the CBD for employment or for the services it offers.

The solid lines represent migration, i.e. permanent movements of population which involve a change of residence. Migration takes place as the result of personal evaluation of:

push factors – unfavourable conditions in the place of origin that encourage movement away;

pull factors – the perceived attractions of the destination.

Migration occurs when the combined effects of push and pull factors are strong enough to overcome the friction of the cost and the difficulty of the movement and change of residence involved.

Different types of migration are indicated on the model.

Line 2 represents migration to new and expanded towns,

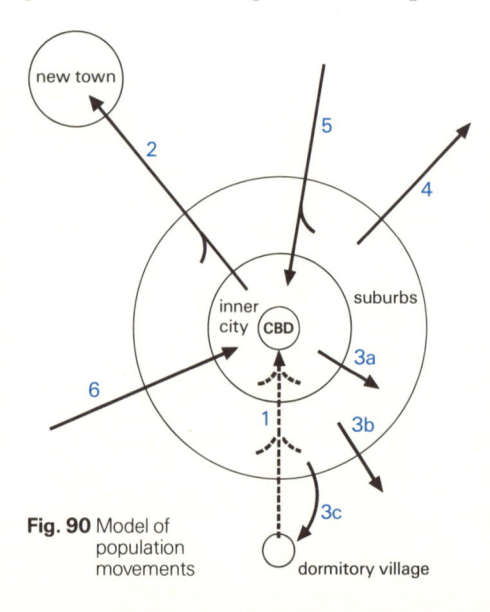

Fig. 90 Model of population movements

pulled largely by employment opportunities in new factories and offices, and by higher-quality housing.

Lines 3a, 3b and 3c together represent a steady outward movement of population, which leads to expansion of the built-up area. It is caused by the attraction of:
- better housing, more spaciously arranged;
- increasing employment opportunities on the edge of the town.

The steady outward migration of population has led to spatial variation in socio-economic class. It is the higher groups – managers, professional people, etc. – who generally have the income to afford higher housing costs and lengthy journeys to work. Inner-city areas tend to have above-average proportions of semi-skilled and unskilled groups.

Note that recently there has been a slight reversal of the trend of outward migration, as wealthier people move into high-cost prestige redevelopments in or near the city centre (London Docklands, Salford Quays). Line 4 represents migration out of the urban area on retirement, e.g. from Greater London to Devon or the South Coast.

Line 5 represents movement into the town by people from rural areas, perhaps 'pushed' by loss of employment in farming and 'pulled' by jobs and services of the town.

The arrow marked 6 represents immigration from overseas. Throughout history, the UK has received waves of immigrants from overseas. In post-war years the origins of the majority of immigrants have been the 'New Commonwealth' countries, particularly those of the Caribbean (e.g. Jamaica) and south-east Asia (e.g. Bangladesh, Pakistan). It has given rise to multi-cultural communities within many large urban areas. The migration was prompted mainly by contrasts in employment opportunities, especially in the 1950s, but sometimes by religious or political persecution (e.g. Ugandan Asians in 1972).

Immigrants tend to concentrate in inner-city areas, with different ethnic groups clustering in different parts. This is because:
a) immigrants generally arrive with few resources and, being unable to purchase housing, start low on council waiting-lists. Therefore they must take advantage of relatively low-cost rented accommodation that may be available in inner cities (perhaps as a result of movement 3a);
b) they can provide mutual help, e.g. with language and cultural problems;
c) there is the advantage of being close to cultural facilities, e.g. mosque, temple, shop, etc.

Note that the UK concentration of ethnic groups is seldom more than 20% of the total population of an area, and never reaches the degree of dominance found in the "ghettos" of New York City, for instance.

Urban Problems in Developed Countries

These are varied and become more acute with increasing size. They are seen at their most serious in the world's major conurbations – London, Paris, Tokyo, New York, etc.

Movement

Increased populations, making longer and more frequent journeys for work and pleasure, often in private vehicles, lead to great congestion on a pattern of roads that, for the most part, was developed in the nineteenth century or earlier. Great efforts are made to ease the problem. London's orbital motorway (M25) diverts through traffic away from central London, but can itself become congested. Other common measures can be illustrated with Paris:
- the removal of produce markets (Les Halles), the source of much traffic, from the centre of Paris to the suburbs;
- the construction of the boulevard périphérique – a high-speed ring road around the centre of Paris;
- the extension of the underground railway (the Métro) and the construction of a new high-speed addition to the network (RER). Fares on the Métro are kept low;
- the building of new towns to accommodate overspill population away from Paris.

Note that in towns generally, the CBD shows signs of the conflict between the advantages of accessibility and the problem of congestion:
- parking restrictions and meters;
- high-rise car-parks on the fringe of the CBD;
- pedestrianisation of shopping streets.

Inner-City Environment

In many instances, this gives cause for great concern. Problems include:
- housing is often old and, where still waiting refurbishment, lacking in basic amenities;
- post-war redevelopment has sometimes led to high-rise or 'system-built' accommodation which has proved disappointing. Flats may be damp, lacking in sound insulation, structurally unsound, etc.;
- the decline of manufacturing industry in central parts of cities leads to high levels of local unemployment;
- there is a lack of open spaces and recreational facilities;
- there are likely to be social problems, e.g. vandalism, street violence, drugs, etc.

Ethnic minorities may experience additional problems:
- language difficulties may hinder the acquisition of skills, and unemployment runs at a very high level;

- racial discrimination and conflict may hinder integration.

Governments attempt to alleviate the problems by encouraging:
- housing improvement;
- the establishment of new industry (Enterprise Zones);
- conversion of old facilities to new uses, e.g.:
stations to art galleries (Paris) or exhibition centres (Manchester) markets to shops, restaurants, etc. (Convent Garden, London, and Les Halles, Paris).

Pollution

Various types of pollution are associated with the city:
- noise – from various sources, but especially road traffic;
- visual – litter, dereliction;
- atmospheric – especially from car exhausts. In the local relief conditions of Los Angeles, car fumes give rise to frequent and serious petrochemical smog.

Urban Expansion and the Green Belt

With rising population and the popularity of low-density housing, there is a danger that urban areas may 'sprawl' loosely outwards to ever-expanding distances from the centre. The *green belt* is an attempt to check this. It is a designated zone of farmland around the built-up area, in which planning controls strictly limit development so that:
- a limit is imposed on the size (area) of a large town;
- the merging of cities (e.g. Birmingham/Coventry) is prevented;
- open land is retained within easy reach of the population.

The green belt idea has critics, who point out that:
- restriction of expansion leads to a rise in the price of land and hence of house prices;
- development leap-frogs the green belt, causing expansion of towns and villages, and lengthening the daily journey to work for many;
- green belt land is farmland and hence of limited public access;
- any poor-quality land in the green belt is preserved in agriculture, when it would be better used for other purposes.

New Towns

New towns, world-wide, may be developed for a variety of purposes, e.g. administrative (Brasilia) and mining (Schefferville, Canada). Of more significance to GCSE examinations, however, are those developed in the post-war UK, because of:

1. the need for new houses, due to bomb damage and a lack of building during the war years;

2. the need to accommodate populations displaced when inner-city areas were redeveloped to lower densities (overspill);
3. a general desire to improve housing conditions, and to prevent unlimited expansion of existing towns and cities.

New towns may differ in detail, but characteristics common to many include:
- located relatively close to (but distinct from) their parent conurbation (Stevenage – London, Skelmersdale – Merseyside);
- planned to be self-contained in terms of employment, services, etc.;
- of restricted size – all houses within reach of both employment and open countryside;
- carefully designed to give a good living environment. Characteristics are:
  i) separation of housing and industry;
  ii) quality housing in well-planned, attractive neighbourhoods with low-order service centre;
  iii) low housing density;
  iv) separation, as far as possible, of pedestrians and traffic;
  v) range of functions available in CBD;
  vi) parks, open spaces, and other recreational facilities.

Not all new towns are judged to have been unqualified successes. Many have not reached the population size that was planned. Problems identified in new towns include:
- the difficulty of creating a community from scratch;
- an unbalanced population structure;
- the relatively high cost of housing;
- an economic depression bringing decline to the area with associated problems of unemployment;
- an unfavourable image which has deterred people from moving in;
- the development of commuting to the parent conurbation.

Today, the tendency is not for new towns to be developed on green field sites, but for established towns to have planned expansion (e.g. Swindon, Peterborough).

Urbanisation

Urbanisation means the increasing proportion of the population that lives within urban areas. In the nineteenth and early twentieth centuries, following the Industrial Revolution, urbanisation was pronounced in Europe and North America. The population living in towns commonly came to represent more than 75% of the total. In these countries, urbanisation has passed its peak. There is now, in many advanced countries, a distinct balance of movement from town to country (commuters, retirement, etc.). This is known as *counter-urbanisation*.

Today, urbanisation is a feature of many Third World areas, such as those of South America and Africa. It is worth noting that it is the largest cities (often the capitals) that are growing at the greatest rate. The world total of cities with a population of a million is expanding rapidly, as is the number of cities with multi-million populations. The increase is greatest in the Third World.

The reasons for Third World urbanisation are:
- high natural increase of population in existing urban populations;
- strong inward flow of migrants from the countryside.

This migration is the result of evaluation of the following 'push' and 'pull' factors:

Push factors – encouraging movement away from the countryside.
1. Rural unemployment and poverty caused by:
   a) rapid population increase;
   b) subdivision of plots below subsistence size;
   c) increased use of machines reducing the demand for wage labour.
2. Declining productivity of land – soil erosion.
3. Natural hazards and the famine that may follow.
4. Rural indebtedness.
5. War (e.g. southern Sudan).

Pull factors – attracting migration to the cities.
1. Greater opportunities for employment.
2. Greater availability of services, e.g. health care and education.
3. Social and entertainment amenities, e.g. cinema.

Note that the 'pull' is what the intending immigrant perceives to be the situation in the destination. He or she may well be disappointed on arrival.

Rapid urbanisation brings to towns such as Calcutta a range of extremely serious problems, some of which are listed below.
- Lack of housing, leading to:
   i) overcrowding in existing accommodation, often of poor quality to begin with;
   ii) rapid growth of 'shanty towns' (known as *bustees* in India), which are of the flimsiest construction and lack the most basic amenities such as piped water and sewage;
   iii) street living.
- Very high rate of unemployment (and part-time employment at very low wages) – hence poverty, which, together with poor living conditions, leads to malnutrition and ill health generally.
- Rising crime rate.
- Unbalanced population structure, for the immigrant stream is

Third World Problems · Points to Note

dominated by males aged between 15 and 35.

Third World countries attempt to cope with the problems, but the scale may overwhelm the meagre resources that can be made available. Nevertheless, efforts are made in the following directions:
- Encouragement of birth control.
- Planned housing improvements and improved health services.
- Industrial development to provide employment.
- Rural development to check the pressure for migration.

Points to Note

1. Be sure that you can distinguish between:
   a) site and situation;
   b) settlement and settlement pattern;
   c) growth of towns and urbanisation.
2. The term 'land use' simply means the use made of the land. On an air photograph of a CBD, for instance, you will be able to identify several types of land use, e.g. shops, offices, roads, car-parks, transport, churches, etc.
3. Note, and be prepared to describe and suggest reasons for, changes in the city with distance from the centre. Examples include:
   a) street plans and house types;
   b) land values;
   c) population density;
   d) socio-economic class.
4. The great majority of us live in, or are familiar with, a large urban area. These differ in detail but have common characteristics, problems, and attempted solutions. Don't hesitate to quote examples from your own experience. If you live in Coventry, for instance, you will appreciate that your city's Ringway is a match (in purpose, if not in size) for the boulevard périphérique of Paris.
5. It is worth emphasising that the city is constantly changing. Make a note of the changes – and their consequences – that are taking place in your urban area. Common illustrations include:
   a) functions such as shops, manufacturing and offices move outwards from the centre as they seek the advantages of the periphery – lower land costs, less congestion, more attractive environment, etc.;
   b) developments in one part of the CBD may lead to a decline in others;
   c) new transport developments.
6. Links are commonly forged between topics featured in this chapter, and OS maps (and photographs, too). Examples include:

Points to Note

    a)   settlement, site and situation;
    b)   how the nature of the land has influenced urban expansion (e.g. avoidance of ill-drained land and steep slopes);
    c)   urban morphology – the pattern of house types and street patterns;
    d)   identification of urban function.

7. Apply your knowledge of the factors influencing industry (page 74) to the situation in the large urban area (page 99).

8. A useful exercise is to compare and contrast the characteristics and problems of a large urban area in an advanced country with one in the Third World.

12 Population

Population Density

Population density is simply the number of people per unit area. For instance, in rounded figures, 56 147 000 people live on the UK's 244 100 square kilometres. Division of the number of people by the area gives a population density of 230 per km^2.

A glance at the appropriate atlas map reveals that on a world scale, population density shows great variations, i.e. the world's population is very unevenly distributed. Within a varied picture, areas of very low and very high density stand out clearly.

For explanations, frequently requested, two groups of factors should be considered:

1. Variations of resources offered by differing environments. These include climate and soils, as well as fuels and minerals. Remember that the bulk of the world's population depends directly or indirectly on agriculture for its livelihood.

2. A wide range of human factors which influence a population's ability to take advantage of the opportunities offered by the environment. These factors include skills and technology, availability of capital, cultural traditions and Government policies.

Major areas of very low population density (less than 5 per km^2) correspond closely to the world's hostile environments, such as arctic, boreal forests, deserts and mountains. For one or more reasons of unfavourable temperature, growing season, rainfall, slope and soil etc., they offer few, if any, agricultural opportunities. Other opportunities – mineral deposits, for example – are few; and development is usually hampered by remoteness and lack of transport.

Areas of high density fall into two groups:

1. Europe, N. America, Japan – where, on a basis of advanced agriculture, exploitation of natural resources and/or the development of a high level of technology has led to considerable growth in industry and the services it supports.

2. Land occupied by mainly agricultural populations in parts of south-east Asia, such as the flood-plains and deltas of India and China. Here the environment offers opportunities for highly-intensive agriculture – the typical family is supported on a tiny patch of land. Note that these densities are achieved at the price of a low average standard of living.

Population density varies at all scales. Again, from your atlas, note the contrasts within the UK – between the Highlands of Scotland and the Central Valley of the same country, for instance. Consideration of relative opportunities is a basis for explanation.

To take another much smaller-scale example, density varies within large urban areas, reflecting the differences in the sizes, styles and spacing of housing accommodation.

Be careful not to equate levels of population density with the concepts of overpopulation and underpopulation. *Overpopulation* occurs when the population of a country or an area is considered too large for the resources and technology available. Poverty, unemployment, malnutrition and emigration are signs of overpopulation. A low standard of living will fall even lower should population continue to increase. Bangladesh, with an average population of 710 per km^2, is often quoted as an example. It is important to note that even an area with a low population density, such as much of the African Sahel, may be overpopulated, for the resources and opportunities of the region are very few. *Underpopulation* is the reverse – too few people to make full and effective use of the resources of a region. Australia and the prairies of Canada are examples. Many consider that the same is true of the Amazon Basin, and this has encouraged the recent developments in the region, with the consequences considered on page 90.

Population Change

Fig. 91 Population data for selected countries

	Total Population Millions	Population Density (per km^2)	Birth Rate ‰	Death Rate ‰	Annual rate of population increase %	Infant mortality	Life expectancy	% of population 0–14
USA	242	25	16	9	0.5	10	73	22
USSR	281	12	20	10	1.0	25	71	25
FRANCE	56	101	14	10	0.5	8	75	21
JAPAN	122	323	11	6	0.5	5	76	23
SWEDEN	9	18	13	11	0.2	6	76	18
UK	57	228	13	11	0.2	9	74	20
BRAZIL	139	16	19	6	1.3	49	64	37
INDIA	767	230	33	12	2.1	104	56	37
BANGLADESH	101	710	44	18	2.6	128	47	46
GHANA	15	58	47	15	3.2	98	47	47
KENYA	22	35	55	14	4.1	80	41	53
PERU	20	16	36	10	2.6	90	59	41

Fig. 91 gives statistics for a selection of countries.

Birth Rate is the number of live births per 1000 (‰) of the population per year.

Death Rate is the number of deaths per 1000 of the population per year.

The difference between these rates, expressed as a percentage, gives a measure of change. Today, in virtually every country, birth rate is greater than death rate. Change is positive; population is increasing. The rate of increase varies. The figures quoted in Fig. 91 look low, deceptively low,

Demographic Transition Model

but bear in mind that a 2% rate of increase means that a country's population doubles in 35 years. Many countries record a rate of increase of 2% or more. As a result, world population is increasing very rapidly. We speak of a population 'explosion'. This is emphasised by the curve of the graph of estimated world population (Fig. 92). As the statistics in Fig. 91 reveal, increase is far from uniform. It is low in developed countries (e.g. the UK) but high, often very high, in less developed countries such as Kenya or Ghana.

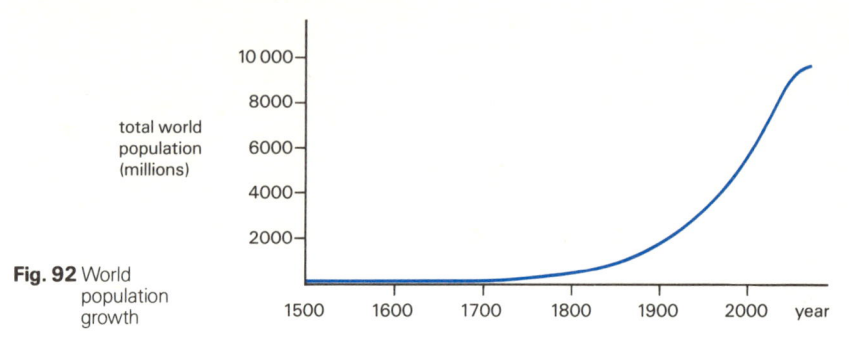

Fig. 92 World population growth

Demographic Transition Model

Birth and Death rates vary with time. Fig. 93 illustrates the *demographic transition model*, which suggests that there is a pattern to these changes. It emphasises the relationship between birth and death rates and total population. Note that the model is divided into four stages.

Stage I

Birth rate is high for reasons that include the following:

1. infant mortality is high and parents desire many births to ensure the survival of sufficient offspring (especially male) to:
   a) help work the land – even young children may be an economic asset;
   b) provide security in old age;
2. larger families are regarded as a sign of male potency;
3. religious beliefs may influence family size;
4. people may lack knowledge of contraception.

Death rate, too, is high because of:

1. disease, encouraged by inadequate diet, impure water and poor hygiene;
2. few medical facilities;
3. war and natural hazards.

Note from the model that total population fluctuates, but on average changes little. Bangladesh is a good example.

Demographic Transition Model

Fig. 93 Demographic transition model

Birth and Death rates ‰ per year

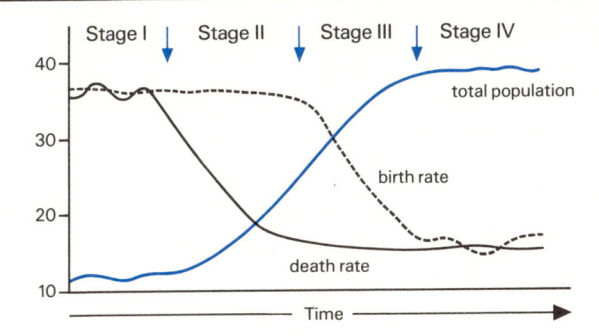

Stage I | Stage II | Stage III | Stage IV

total population
birth rate
death rate

Time →

Stage II
Birth rate is high (same reasons as in Stage I), but death rate declines steeply with time, because of:
1. advances in medical science, e.g. new drugs;
2. improved health care, e.g. innoculation and clinics, which help bring about a significant reduction in the *infant mortality rate* – the number of deaths of infants under the age of one year, per 1000 live births per year;
3. improved hygiene – sanitation, water supply, etc.

With a falling death rate, total population increases dramatically. Examples of countries considered to be in this stage of the model today include Peru, Ghana and Zaire.

Stage III
Death rate continues to fall, but at a generally lower rate. Birth rate falls. Several factors may contribute to this:
1. lower infant mortality – more children survive, therefore reduced economic need for large families;
2. encouragement of family planning – education, and the provision of the means of contraception;
3. changes in the position of women in many societies;
4. greater desire for material possessions.

Total population continues to rise, but at a progressively lower rate. Argentina may be quoted as an example.

Stage IV
Birth rate and death rate are both low, the reasons being extensions of those in Stages II and III. Total population shows little change. Sweden, the UK and most countries of Western Europe are considered to be in this stage.

A possible fifth stage, when death rate is greater than birth rate and population declines, is suggested by recent experience in one or two advanced countries in Western Europe. An example might be West Germany.

Population Structure

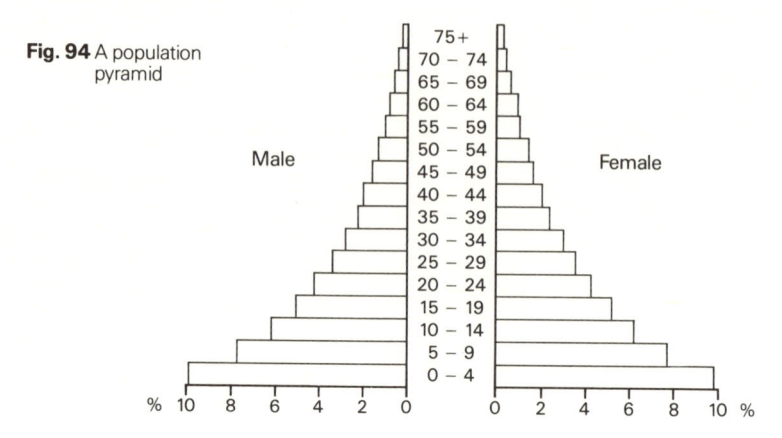

Fig. 94 A population pyramid

[Population pyramid showing Male (left) and Female (right) with age groups from 0–4 at base to 75+ at top, in 5-year intervals: 0–4, 5–9, 10–14, 15–19, 20–24, 25–29, 30–34, 35–39, 40–44, 45–49, 50–54, 55–59, 60–64, 65–69, 70–74, 75+. Horizontal axis shows % from 0 to 10 on each side.]

The structure of a population is its composition by age and sex. It is usually illustrated by means of a graph known as a *population pyramid* – an example is given as Fig. 94. Bars represent percentages of population within stated age and sex groups. With the passage of time, each group naturally gets older, and, of course, smaller as death takes its toll. Reflecting this, the bars get progressively shorter, until finally a group is no more and disappears from the pyramid, for which new births provide a new base.

That part of the population that is between 15 and 65 is described as *economically active*. The remainder, young and elderly, are described as *dependent*. Dependency ratio is the total of the dependent population divided by the number of economically active. It varies considerably from country to country.

Population structure, reflecting as it does changes in birth and death rates, itself changes with time. Stages of the demographic transition model have characteristic shapes. A generalised example, typical of Stage II, is given as Fig. 95. A high birth rate gives a wide base to the pyramid. Death rate, although declining, is still high, hence the sloping sides. Life expectancy is low, and so the percentage of the population over 65 is small. Problems commonly experienced by countries with this structure (i.e. countries at Stage II) include:
- increasing pressure on:
    i) resources, e.g. land;
    ii) services, e.g. education;
- unemployment – declining living standards;
- poverty – malnutrition;
- meeting the needs of dependent young, e.g. education – 40% or more of the population may be less than 15 years old;
- too rapid urbanisation.

Population Pyramid

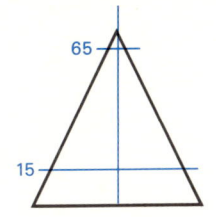

Fig. 95 Generalised shape of a population pyramid for Stage II of the demographic transition model

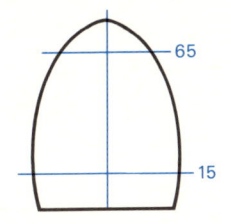

Fig. 96 Generalised shape of a population pyramid for Stage IV of the demographic transition model

Efforts made to reduce the birth rate in developing countries include:
- education;
- raising of living standards;
- propaganda;
- provision of means of birth control;
- laws to control the age of marriage and family size.

The demographic transition model suggests that, in time, the structure illustrated by Fig. 95 will change to that represented by Fig. 96, a shape that represents the population structure of many advanced countries. The narrow base to the pyramid is due to a low birth rate. The steep sides reflect a low death rate, and with people on average living longer, there is a large percentage of the population over 65. A country with this population structure may also have the following problems:
- a large and increasing number of elderly people must be supported and cared for;
- a declining proportion of economically active people may be unable to support the social services;
- future labour shortages threaten the economy.

Other relatively minor influences on population structure which may be identified on pyramids are:
- major wars – deficit of population in certain age groups due to death and reduction in the number of births;
- migration – the receiving area will show a projection of those bars representing the dominant sex and age groups in the migration stream (usually young adult males). There is a reverse effect on the structure of the area of origin. Note that international migration is generally too low to have these effects. Jamaica, however, is an exception. It can be very significant within countries (e.g. rural to urban migration in Third World countries);
- introduction of birth-control policy – a sharp narrowing of the base of the pyramid;
- greater longevity of women – the pyramid bulges on the female side above 65.

Population Movement

Fig. 97 Types of population movement

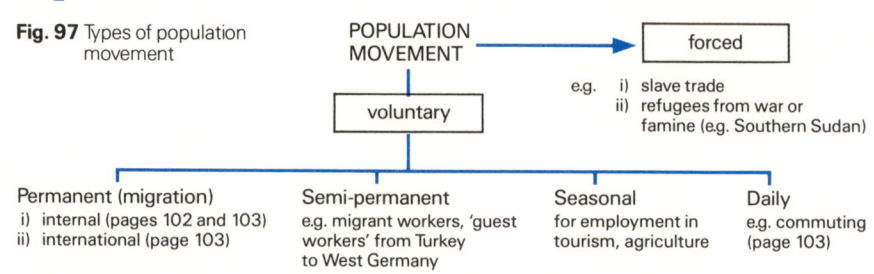

```
                    POPULATION  ─────────▶  forced
                    MOVEMENT
                         │         e.g.  i) slave trade
                         ▼               ii) refugees from war or
                     voluntary               famine (e.g. Southern Sudan)
```

Permanent (migration)	Semi-permanent	Seasonal	Daily
i) internal (pages 102 and 103) ii) international (page 103)	e.g. migrant workers, 'guest workers' from Turkey to West Germany	for employment in tourism, agriculture	e.g. commuting (page 103)

The major types of population movement are indicated in Fig. 97. Note that permanent movements (migrations) are not undertaken lightly, especially if distance is great. Cost may be a major obstacle. Then the loss of contact with family and friends must be considered. So, too, must the uncertainties of life in a new and different environment and culture. These considerable obstacles must be outweighed by the perceived advantages of migration based on evaluation of push and pull factors before movement takes place.

All migrations are different and have differing consequences. For instance, since the end of the Second World War, West Germany has attracted immigrants ('gastarbeiter') from many countries, especially Turkey. This flow was originally only semi-permanent, but many settled, and today West Germany has a Turkish community of over 5 million. The main consequences of this migration are summarised below.

TURKEY	WEST GERMANY
Advantages	
1. reduction of unemployment. 2. reduced pressure on resources, e.g. land. 3. money sent home by migrants – major source of foreign exchange.	1. solves labour shortage, especially for dirty, unskilled, ill-paid, but essential jobs.
Disadvantages	
1. loss of skills. 2. majority of migrants young and male – population structure unbalanced.	1. unbalanced population structure. 2. concentration of migrants in areas of low-standard housing. 3. racial tension. 4. in times of depression, migrants lose jobs – pressure on social services.

Points to Note

1. The following are terms to be clearly appreciated: population density, birth and death rates, rate of population change, dependency ratio.

2. For a major area of low population density (high mountains, deserts, boreal forests, etc.), suggest reasons why it should support so few people. The list of factors influencing agriculture is a good starting-point, for, if they are unfavourable, agricultural opportunities are naturally limited. Similar use can be made of the factors influencing industry.

3. Likewise, know the reasons why a selected region supports a high density of population.

4. The demographic transition model is popular with examiners. Can you draw Fig. 93 from memory? Aim to be clear about the changes that take place from stage to stage and be ready with explanation.

5. In the manner illustrated on page 116, be ready to analyse the consequences of other migrations that you have studied.

13 Development Issues

'North' and 'South' – the First, Second and Third Worlds

Fig. 98 World contrasts

Examples of NICs:	Examples of OPEC countries:	(Exception)
1 South Korea	3 Saudi Arabia	6 Republic of South Africa
2 Taiwan	4 Iraq	(because of political/racial structure)
	5 Libya	

(shaded area = centrally-planned economies)

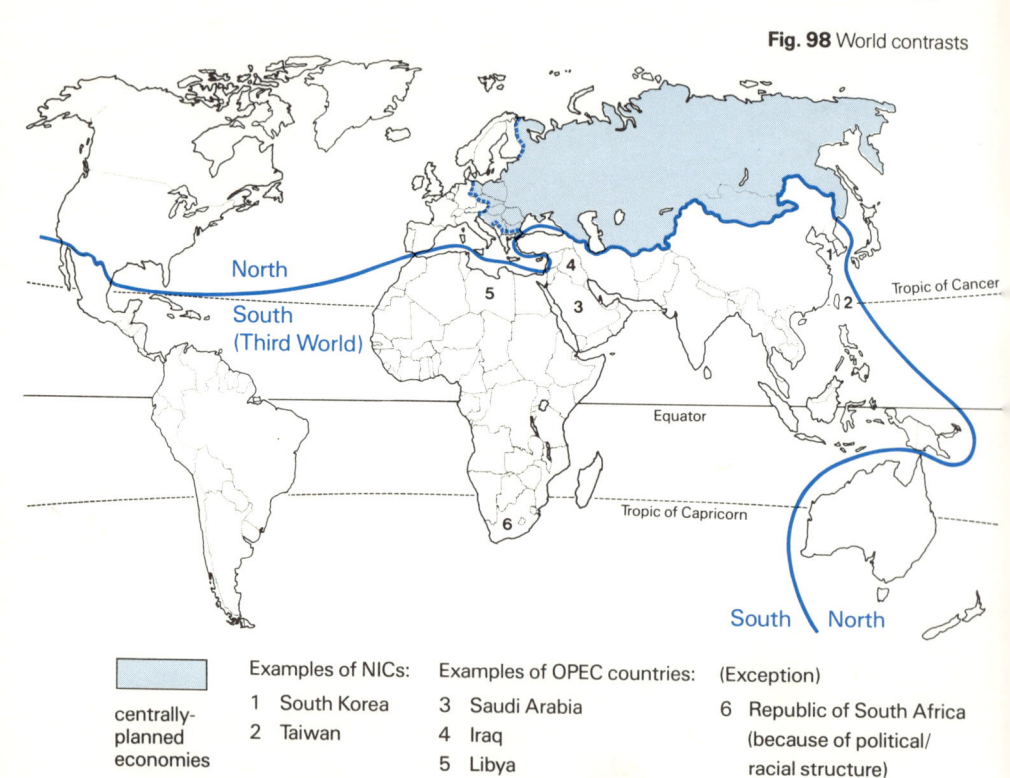

Fig. 98 illustrates a fundamental division of the world's many diverse countries. A confusing variety of names is in use.

The 'North', or developed/industrialised world, is made up of More Developed Countries (MDCs). The North is subdivided into the *First World* of market (*capitalist*) economies and the *Second World* of centrally-planned (*communist*) economies.

The 'South' is composed of Less Developed Countries (LDCs). The South is also known as the 'developing world' or, more commonly, as the *Third World*. Note that it includes centrally-planned economies such as China and Cuba.

The distinction between North and South is made on the evidence of a wide range of statistical indicators, a selection of which is given in Fig. 99.

Evaluation of Development

Fig. 99 Indicators of development

[1] net material profit (best communist equivalent)
[2] private vehicles only

	Gross National Product per capita (US $)	Energy consumption (kg per capita coal equivalent)	% of work-force employed in agriculture	Urban population (%)	Population per doctor	Adult literacy rate	Motor vehicles No. in use per 1000 p.p.
USA	16 690	9489	3	74	549	>99	714
USSR	2588[1]	6389	26	65	267	>99	45[2]
FRANCE	9540	3881	7	73	483	>99	439
JAPAN	11 300	3625	9	77	735	>99	371
SWEDEN	11 890	4893	5	83	478	>99	396
UK	8460	5363	2	92	670	>99	338
BRAZIL	1640	761	30	72	1647	74	86
INDIA	270	272	63	25	2545	64	3
BANGLADESH	130	62	58	12	8988	25	1
GHANA	380	96	48	32	7245	30	7
KENYA	290	78	75	20	9900	47	13
PERU	1010	524	38	67	1442	72	31

NB. See Fig. 91, page 111, for other indicators of development, i.e. birth rate, rate of population increase, % of pop < 15, etc.

Gross National Product (GNP) is the sum total of the value, measured in US Dollars ($), of all the goods and services produced in a country in a year. Division by the number of people in the country gives *GNP per head* (or per capita). This is the most frequently used indicator of a country's wealth and development; but there are reservations that must be borne in mind:

- There are difficulties in collecting data, and countries differ in their methods of accounting.
- Subsistence production is not included.
- A national average figure for GNP per head hides great contrasts in wealth between region and region, and between social groups.
- Money is only one aspect of development. GNP per head is best used in association with other indicators.

Evaluation of development is by no means easy. The diverse indicators must often be treated with caution. However, a clear development gap can be recognised between rich and poor countries, between North and South. These, it must be stressed, are not groupings of identical countries. Within each there is great diversity, e.g. in the South we find contrasts as great as those between Mexico and Ethiopia.

Note the following points:

- Some states within the area mapped as South have experienced marked industrial development in recent decades. Examples include Taiwan, Singapore and South Korea. They are known as Newly Industrialised Countries (NICs).
- The GNP of some states – Saudi Arabia and Kuwait, for instance – is boosted by oil wealth, and they score less well on other indicators.

Characteristic Features of LDCs

1. *Low GNP per capita.* The figure is often less than $500. (The UK figure is more than ten times this.)

2. *Uneven distribution of wealth.* In many LDCs, a small, rich minority usually controls the greater part of land and other economic resources.

3. *Shortage of capital.* In a poor country, where the bulk of the population is totally concerned with the day-to-day needs of survival, it is difficult for money to be put aside as capital for future development. Remember that capital – money for investment – is essential for all forms of development. The lack of capital is a factor in the next two points.

4. *Low level of social provision* in, for example:
   a) *health* – poor medical provision plus poor diet (often malnutrition) help to explain poor health and low life expectancy;
   b) *education* – low level of literacy. People find it difficult to acquire the knowledge and skills needed for development.

5. *Lack of infrastructure,* e.g. transport and power services, which is vital to the development of both agriculture and industry.

6. *The economy (hence employment) is dominated by primary activity,* especially agriculture. Manufacturing and service industries are poorly developed.

7. *Export trade is dominated by a small number of primary products* – raw materials or food crops. The foreign currency earned by these exports pays for essential imports, such as fuel, machinery, fertilisers, etc. In recent years the prices of primary products on world markets have fallen, and the costs of manufactured imports have risen. The 'terms of trade', as the economists say, have moved against the LDCs, to the detriment of their hopes of development.

8. *Population structure.* Many Third World countries are in Stage II of the demographic transition. They have high birth rates, falling death rates and hence a rapidly increasing population, with a very high percentage of the population below 15 years of age. In many LDCs, the population grows more rapidly than the economy, so the GNP per head declines. The country becomes poorer and the standard of living declines.

9. *Indebtedness.* Many LDCs have borrowed large sums from the rich countries of the North to finance development schemes. Rates of interest are high, and repayment has posed problems. So, many LDCs are in debt and a large slice of national income, badly needed for development, must go to rich lending countries of the North as interest and repayment of debt.

Problems of Agriculture in the 'South'

A powerful group of factors contributes to low state of development in countries of the South.

Environmental Factors

Most LDCs lie within tropical latitudes. Environments pose varied and serious difficulties, such as:
- large areas where rainfall is too low or too unreliable for productive agriculture;
- markedly seasonal rainfall in other large regions. Monsoon rains may, for instance, arrive too late, or be too light for good crops;
- tropical soils, e.g. those of the tropical rain forest, often of very low fertility;
- natural hazards, e.g. floods, drought, tropical storms. These set back progress. Farmers at or near subsistence level have no reserves to fall back on. To make a new start, farmers must borrow from a money-lender at a high rate of interest.

Landholding

The varied systems often do not encourage progress or development of agriculture:
- large estates, often with absentee landlords, worked extensively by wage labour on low wages, seasonal labour;
- share-cropping – tenant farmer has no security, and little incentive to make improvements;
- small size of individual holdings – little if any surplus, no capital for development.

Population Pressure

Rapid growth of population in areas of subsistence agriculture gives rise to problems. Higher population leads to increased demand for food and:
- overstocking of grazing land, and the destruction of vegetation. In dry years this may lead to desertification;
- reduction in the period of fallow in an arable farm economy, with a resultant decline in soil fertility;
- on the death of a farmer, division of the landholding among his sons into plots too small to support a family.

Low Level of Literacy

This restricts the spread of new farming ideas, crops and techniques.

Poor Infrastructure

Transport facilities are poor and marketing opportunities limited. Farmers may have difficulty in selling any surplus crops which they may produce.

Lack of Capital

This restricts all aspects of agricultural improvement from the purchase of fertilisers to the breeding of improved stock.

Poverty and Development

In view of the problems, it is not surprising that many LDCs, and many individual farmers, are trapped in what is described as the vicious circle of poverty (Fig. 100).

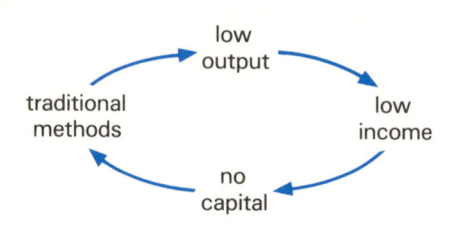

Fig. 100 The vicious circle of poverty

The aim of development is to break the circle. The injection of capital can lead to basic improvements such as new crops, selected seeds, fertilisers, water supply, easier credit, transport and marketing facilities. All these may contribute to improved output and the production of a surplus. The sale of this in turn is used to create more capital for more improvements, more output, more capital, and so on. The vicious circle of agricultural poverty may thus be converted into an upward spiral of development.

Hoping to make this change, LDCs may augment their very limited domestic sources of capital through:
- international agencies such as the International Monetary Fund or the World Bank – loans available at low rates of interest;
- commercial banks in the rich countries of Western Europe and North America – loans at commercial rates of interest;
- investments by multinational companies;
- grants or loans between countries North and South;
- charities such as Oxfam, Save the Children Fund, etc., which work for development as well as disaster relief.

Note that for many agricultural developments the supply of expertise (agricultural and veterinary scientists, engineers and hydrologists, for example) is as important as cash.

The list of possible sources of capital looks long, but many people consider that the level of aid given by MDCs (especially aid which does not carry high rates of interest) is inadequate for the needs of the LDCs.

Development Strategies

Agricultural development in LDCs may be sought in a variety of ways. A number of illustrations follow.

Major Capital-Intensive Projects

Egypt's Aswan High Dam, for instance, created a reservoir which provides irrigation water for nearly a quarter of a million hectares of new farmland. The scheme also provides for the generation of much hydroelectric power. These are tremendous gains, but there are disadvantages:
- the silt which once fertilised the fields of lower Egypt now slowly silts up the reservoir;
- much moisture is lost from the surface of the reservoir by evaporation in the hot desert climate;
- repayment of the loan to the USSR made heavy demands on the benefits of increased production.

Small-Scale Labour-Intensive Schemes

These schemes are found in many Third World countries. They involve the development, improvement, or increase in security, of traditional agriculture methods. They make little demand on scarce capital or expensive energy. Many of the schemes involve the cultivators in guided self-help – e.g. the ridging of sloping croplands to encourage the infiltration of rainfall, and to reduce the risk of soil erosion. Ridging is achieved by hoe, rather than by high-technology earth-moving equipment.

The schemes often make use of *'alternative'* or *'intermediate' technology* – wind-driven, rather than diesel-driven, pumps for irrigation water; new steel ploughs drawn by oxen, rather than fuel-thirsty tractors. Such schemes are often introduced by development charities. The spread of new ideas, methods and skills by trained local example is an important feature. Progress is hard and slow, but cheaper, surer and steadier than some of the more elaborate capital-intensive schemes of development.

Social Reorganisation

An example of social reorganisation is the Ujamaa (Swahili for family) scheme of Tanzania. This has the twin aims of:
1. increased agricultural output;
2. provision of services such as health and education.

To achieve these aims, it was necessary to collect a formerly dispersed agricultural population into new villages and promote communal ownership of the land. Village committees now plan production with the help of Government and World Bank funding.

Provision of services in the new Ujamaa villages represents great improvement in the standard of living of the people, but agricultural progress is considered by many to be disappointing. A commonly suggested reason is the lack of personal incentive to work efficiently on communal land.

Improving Third World Agriculture

The 'Green Revolution'

This is based on the introduction of newly-bred, *high-yielding varieties* (HYVs) of common food grains, such as rice and wheat. These yield two or three times the harvest of traditional varieties, but need to be cultivated as part of a package which includes the regular application of expensive fertilisers and pesticides, and perhaps the careful control of irrigation water.

The consequences have been mixed:
- Substantial increase in output of essential food grains, especially wheat. It has made India and Mexico self-sufficient in food grains.
- Stimulus to the fertiliser and power industries.
- Reduced prices due to increased output – an advantage to the customer but not necessarily to the farmer.
- The application of new techniques, demanding capital and skills. The educated farmer with a large landholding benefits greatly. Small tenant farmers, unable to afford the costs of the Green Revolution, may be driven from the land.

The Opening-Up of New Lands

Unfortunately, these new lands tend to be forested areas of limited agricultural value. The example of Brazil is one area where the consequences of 'development' give great cause for concern.

Industry in the Third World

Manufacturing industry is seen by many as the source of wealth and employment, and the key to future development. But the factors of production considered in Chapter 8 are, in most LDCs, far from favourable.
- *Transport* facilities are poor. Railways are rare. Roads are usually unsurfaced and are dusty or muddy, depending on the season.
- *Power* supplies are extremely limited. The great majority of LDCs lack significant resources of fossil fuels. If potential for HEP is present, lack of capital prevents development in many cases. For power, most LDCs must rely on expensive imports of oil.
- *Labour* force usually lacks essential technical and management skills.
- *Markets* for manufactured products are often tiny, for populations tend to be small and the people poor. With small home markets, industry cannot achieve low unit costs. Products are often much cheaper to import than to produce at home.
- *Capital* is in extremely short supply.

To set against these difficulties, LDCs may have the advantages of:
1. a plentiful supply of unskilled labour for which hours are long and wages low;

2. in some cases, local raw materials, e.g. cotton.

Most LDCs have some traditional, small-scale (craft, cottage) industry, such as the throwing of pots, the hand-weaving of cloth, or the simple processing of agricultural products (palm-oil), etc.

The first steps on the road to industrialisation are usually directed towards import substitution – the manufacture of basic items for the home market, e.g. cloth and clothing, footwear, etc. A small number of LDCs have proceeded further and have moved into manufacture of capital goods, such as machinery and spare parts for use in making and repairing other articles, and consumer durables — manufactured articles for use over lengthy periods by the consumer.

A handful, the newly industrialising countries (NICs), have made great strides and have become centres of manufacturing of world importance. South Korea, for instance, now manufactures steel, ships, cars, electronic equipment, and a very wide range of consumer goods for the home and export markets.

These centres of rapid industrial expansion – Taiwan, Singapore, and others – have prospered because of:

- access to cheap ocean transport, so making it easy to serve markets all over the world;
- low labour costs (less than $1/5$ of those of the UK);
- tax concessions;
- the import and wise use of capital – and the reinvestment of profits;
- investment in education and technical training.

Industrialisation in the Third World is not without its problems, a selection of which are listed.

- Industrialisation may give rise to huge foreign debt.
- Availability of cheap factory products may kill off traditional handicrafts in rural areas, so increasing rural poverty and the movement to the towns.
- New industrial development is often concentrated in one part of a country, usually the capital city – this becomes a 'pull' factor for rural to urban migration.
- Much industrial development is the result of investment by 'Northern' multinational companies. This is criticised by many people, for such companies pay few taxes and profits are taken out of the host country.
- Lack of planning controls may lead to pollution, congestion and poor quality of life.
- Competition from NICs may harm, or perhaps destroy, old-established industries in the advanced countries of the 'North'. Examples in the UK include textiles and shipbuilding.

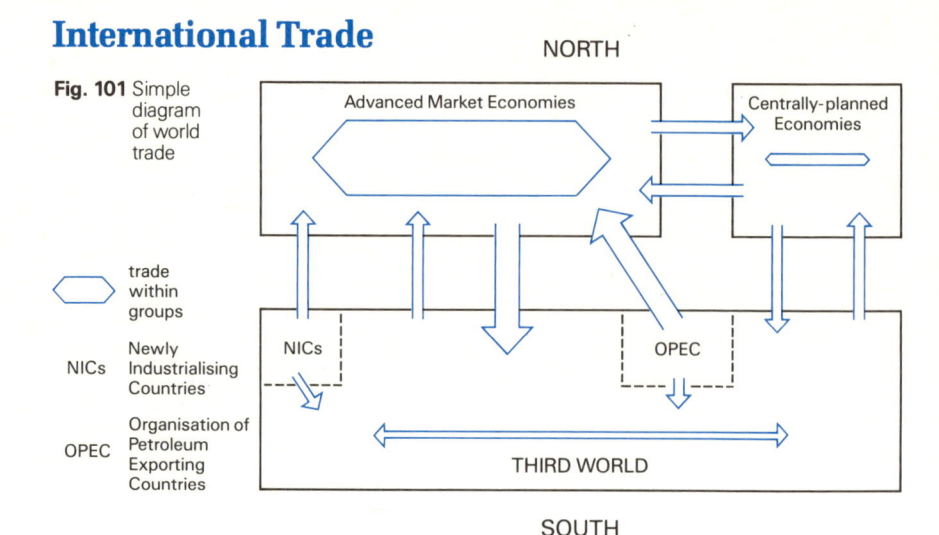

World Trade

International Trade

Fig. 101 Simple diagram of world trade

NORTH / SOUTH

Advanced Market Economies — Centrally-planned Economies — NICs (Newly Industrialising Countries) — OPEC (Organisation of Petroleum Exporting Countries) — THIRD WORLD

trade within groups

Consideration of different types of economically developed countries must not cause us to forget that they are all part of one world, one planet. Countries are linked in a variety of ways, e.g. the United Nations, the Commonwealth, aid (development and military), the work of charities, environmental issues, sport, the media, disaster relief, etc. Of greatest importance, however, is international trade. Fig. 101 illustrates in a very simple, diagrammatic way some of its main features.

• The bulk of world trade is between countries with advanced market economies – North America, Western Europe and Japan. In the main it consists of manufactured goods of all types.

• Second in importance is trade between advanced industrialised countries and the Third World. Basically, the pattern is that the Third World supplies raw materials (e.g. ores, rubber) and foodstuffs (e.g. cocoa, palm-oil), and receives in return manufactured goods such as machinery, chemicals, consumer goods. The cartoon included as Fig. 102 graphically emphasises the importance of this trade to both North and South. In addition to being a source of supply of raw material, the

Fig. 102 One example of the interdependence of 'North' and 'South'

126